Salt in Prehistoric Europe

Sidestone Press

Salt in Prehistoric Europe
Anthony Harding

© 2017 A.F. Harding

First published in 2013 (softcover)

Published by Sidestone Press, Leiden
www.sidestone.com

ISBN 978-90-8890-201-7 (Softcover)
ISBN 978-90-8890-384-7 (Hardcover)
ISBN 978-90-8890-202-4 (PDF e-book)

Printed and bound in Great Britain by
Marston Book Services Ltd, Oxfordshire

Photograph cover:
    front: Salt Crystals, photograph by Paul Looyen, Dreamstime.com
    back: Hallstattersee, Austria, photograph by RoCe, Dreamstime.com

Lay-out & cover design: Sidestone Press

Contents

Preface

This book seeks to set out the current state of play in the study of prehistoric salt-working in Europe, with some consideration of other parts of the world and other periods where these seem to provide information of interest or value to the task in hand. I have tried to avoid simply repeating information that has been frequently presented in the past, though inevitably some of this appears in order to provide the context in which the current situation may be viewed.

The book stems from a long-standing interest in salt on my part, even though my substantial publications on the topic are of relatively recent date and come principally from the fieldwork which Valeriu Cavruc (Valerii Kavruk) and I have conducted in Transylvania over the last 10 years. Since it has sometimes been alleged that I am a newcomer to the field, it is worth pointing out that conference papers in the 1990s considered the matter, as did a section in my book *European Societies in the Bronze Age* (Harding 1998; 2000, 249-254; 2001); these publications appeared just as the current interest in salt was gathering speed, but were written without input from the meetings that were taking place around that time (for instance, they were written several years earlier than a salt session at the EAA Annual Meeting in Esslingen, Germany, in 2001, which I attended).

Now that salt archaeology is an area of study in its own right, many more people are working on the topic. Their writings have inevitably contributed much to what follows in this book. I would particularly like to acknowledge the helpful insights of Olivier Weller (Paris), who knows more about archaeological salt than anyone else and who generously provided offprints on request, Elaine Morris (Southampton), the leader of salt studies in Britain, who has helped me with information on many occasions, and my colleague Valeriu Cavruc (Sfîntu Gheorghe), who has given me unstinting support and intellectual stimulus over many years. For the provision of books and articles over the years, discussions, and invitations to present my material at meetings, I would like to thank Hans Reschreiter and Kerstin Kowarik (Vienna), Alfons Figuls (Cardona), Vassil Nikolov (Sofia), the late lamented Dan Monah (Iaşi), Thomas Saile (Regensburg), Germán Delibes de Castro and Elisa Guerra Doce (Valladolid), Janine Fries-Knoblach (Erlangen), Laurent Olivier (Paris), Cyril Marcigny (Longues-sur-Mer), Gert Goldenberg (Innsbruck), Josip Kobal' (Uzhgorod), Thomas Stöllner (Bochum), Wojciech Blajer (Kraków), Milan Salaš (Brno), Rowan Flad (Harvard), Janice Kinory (Oxford), Jonathan Terán (Zaragoza), Antonio Morgado (Granada), Horia Ciugudean (Alba Iulia), Marc Talon (Croix-Moligneaux), Ian Brown (Tuscaloosa) and David Cranstone (Gateshead).

Special thanks are due to Peter van der Broeke (Nijmegen), who read the entire manuscript in draft, saving me from several errors and making many helpful suggestions, to Eszter Bánffy (Budapest) for helpful comments on Chapter 4, and to Chris Smart (Exeter), who efficiently conducted the GIS study in Chapter 8, collected information on aspects with which I was unfamiliar, and brought together the illustrations, redrawing several of them. The book could not have been brought to fruition without their help. Lastly, the efficient help from Karsten Wentink at Sidestone Press is gratefully acknowledged.

Exeter, UK
August 2013

Chapter 1

Introduction

> *"One may seek less after gold, but there is no one who does not wish to find salt; deservedly so, since every kind of food owes its savour to it"* (Cassiodorus, Variae Epistolae 12.24) (written AD 537/ 538) [1]

The archaeological study of salt in Europe has in recent years seen something of an explosion in interest. In part this is due to a number of remarkable discoveries, in several countries of Europe, and in part to a renewed interest in the commodity as an important element in ancient economies. Especially in the years since 1999 there have been a sizeable number of conferences, seminars and colloquia, resulting in collected volumes, monographs and other publications that have transformed the academic landscape where the study of salt in archaeology is concerned. Many of these publications, or the articles in them, are referenced in this book. A rather small group of scholars have led the way in recent years in the study of salt in prehistory, most notably Olivier Weller (Paris). Their writings, and the meetings and publications they have inspired, have led the way for many others to carry on research into one of the most fundamental, yet intangible, materials encountered in human life. This is not to forget the work of a considerable number of scholars who have made important contributions to the topic, and whose work is considered here.

In many ways this interest is not surprising, since salt is without question important to human societies for a number of reasons, in the present as in the past (see below). Archaeologically, however, salt is difficult to study, since sodium chloride is highly soluble and does not survive when exposed to the elements, or the percolation of water (only one find of actual salt solids appears to be known, that from Kopaka near Zakro in Crete, though pieces of rock salt were discovered in excavation at Pobiednik Wielki near Kraków in southern Poland: below, Chapter 5). This means that salt can – so far – only be studied through the production sites where it was once extracted or created – mines, outcrops, springs, or streams – along with the equipment used for the purpose. Luckily the bacteriocidal action of salt means that organic remains are often preserved in ancient salt production sites, notably wood, but in some cases – such as Hallstatt – leather and textiles. This has in some cases enabled a detailed study of fixed constructions, portable objects, and thus potential techniques for salt production.

---

1 potest aurum aliquis minus quaerere, nemo est qui salem non desideret invenire, merito, quando isti debet omnis cibus quod potest esse gratissimus.

A number of general books, catalogues, articles or edited volumes have appeared in recent years, written for a variety of audiences – ranging from the interested layman to the non-specialist academic (e.g. Adshead 1992; Astrup *et al.* 1993; Bergier 1982; Dopsch *et al.* 1994; Ebenbichler & Ebenbichler 2009; Hocquet 2001; MacGregor & De Wardener 1998; Multhauf 1978; Riera *et al.* 2001). The book by Mark Kurlansky (2002) has attracted considerable attention because of its wide range and easy writing style; while not strictly an academic study, it is nevertheless a treasure trove of information not easily acquired from the academic literature. The books by Robert Multhauf and Jean-François Bergier are likewise highly informative histories of salt production, though for present purposes their concentration on historic periods and reliance on secondary sources makes them less useful.

There are, of course, also a fair number of specialist volumes and articles, many arising from conferences (e.g. Carusi 2008; Daire 2003; Figuls i Alonso & Weller 2007; Monah *et al.* 2007; Vogt 2003; Weller 2002c; Weller *et al.* 2008a), and exhibition catalogues (e.g. Cavruc & Chiricescu 2006; Kull 2003b; Thoen 1990; Treml *et al.* 1995). There are even books that appear to be about salt but in fact have little or nothing to do with it (e.g. Schwaiger 1977; Truong 2003, a novel about Paris in the 1930s). This is to say nothing of the many works that deal with a specific site or area, usually in a specific period (e.g. Kern *et al.* 2009; Lane & Morris 2001; Nikolov 2008; 2009; Prilaux 2000), which will be considered in the various parts of this book.

Some of these books are written by economic historians (e.g. Adshead 1992), some by medical scientists (e.g. Astrup *et al.* 1993), others by historians or popularisers; relatively few general books come from the pen of archaeologists. In general it is wise to be cautious about statements on archaeology and ancient history made by medics, and on biology made by archaeologists; much information is simply repeated from an apparently authoritative source without other checks on validity. A typical example of the former is the chapter on the history of salt in Denton's otherwise important study (1984: 76 ff.), and of the latter Monah's statements about salt biology (2002: 137). Almost all the general books cited above give a very general overview of ancient production, mentioning the briquetage[2] from the Halle region, then moving rapidly to Iron Age sites in Germany and Lorraine, then to medieval and early modern production. The sites of Iron Age France have usually attracted a lot of attention, as has Hallstatt; after all, these were among those first studied, and the term "briquetage" comes from the early French studies. But important as they are, they are not the only important ancient production sites. Apart from anything else, they rely on one technology and concentrate mainly in one period; they have attracted attention because they illustrate vividly a highly developed technology that is in general well understood. So, after a mention of such sites, these general books (several of them written by economic historians) move on

---

2   Briquetage: the coarse ceramic specifically produced for the boiling of salt. For the invention of the term, see below pp. 18, 75.

rapidly to the periods their authors prefer, those with historical records illustrating both the technology and the means of distribution of the finished product.

Most recent authors draw their initial inspiration from the fundamental and pioneering book by Jacques Nenquin (1961), the publication of a Cambridge doctoral thesis which was strongly influenced by Grahame Clark's studies on prehistoric economic life published in a series of articles between the 1930s and 1950s, which also form the basis for his influential book *Prehistoric Europe: the economic basis* (1952), in which chapter 5 had some pages devoted to salt production (Clark 1952, 127-8). Nenquin's work covers almost all of the relevant areas of interest that this work also considers: the location of salt sources, the biological need for salt, the history of research, ethnography, classical, biblical and historical sources, the economic importance of salt in prehistory, and the detail of discoveries in each area of Europe. It is especially useful in its coverage of the history of research, as Nenquin systematically sought out nineteenth century writings in German and French, most of which are little known today; and in its use of classical and biblical sources. These sources are of great interest, and have been cited by many subsequent authors.[3]

Recent spectacular discoveries that shed light on prehistoric production in Europe include those from Austria (Hallstatt, the Dürrnberg near Hallein), France (sites in the Seille vally in Lorraine, especially those near Marsal), Spain (Beaker period production at Vilafáfila near Zamora), Bulgaria (the Neolithic and Eneolithic sites at Provadia inland from Varna), and Romania (Neolithic sites in Moldavia and Bronze Age sites in Transylvania). At the same time, the study of prehistoric salt production has seen renewed interest in Germany, Poland, Italy and Britain, as well as other parts of France – mainly relating to Iron Age (and later) production but in some cases going back to the Bronze Age.

Much remains unknown about how salt was produced, and especially about how it was moved from production area to consumer area or areas. Salt, once mined or turned into crystalline form, is invisible archaeologically. We rely almost entirely on assumptions, based on analogies with historical or ethnographic situations.

The time therefore seems ripe for a general overview of salt in European prehistory, given the remarkable increase in information in recent years, and the advent of new techniques of analysis. Inevitably the treatment of the topic in the pages that follow will pay more attention to some areas than others, but the intention is that all areas and periods should receive enough words to make their importance clear.

The uses of salt

A certain daily intake of salt is needed for human and animal health; and salt has a range of uses in domestic and industrial life, notably for the preservation of foodstuffs through its antimicrobial action.

---

3   It is an interesting commentary on the nature of academic research that each generation discovers such sources for itself, thereby repeating many of the thoughts and understandings of earlier scholars.

The economic historian Michel Mollat had pertinent things to say about salt and its properties, even though archaeology was far from his mind:

> *Sans jouer du paradoxe, le sel est à la fois un produit commun et un produit noble. Un produit commun parce qu'exploité dans le monde entier, sous toutes les formes et de toutes les manières possibles: sel marin par l'évaporation solaire, sel gemme extrait des mines, sel de source par ébullition et concentration, sel de cendre par ébullition, sel résultant du lessivage de certains sols; ces sels ont toujours été utilisés pour la consommation et furent un procédé à peu près unique de conservation pendant des siècles. Noble, le sel l'est par sa valeur vitale, son caractère indispensable à tout être humain; à ce titre, il est considéré comme le symbole même de la force, comme un principe régenerateur purifiant. On pourrait rappeler la formule évangélique du «sel de la terre». Recherché de toute antiquité, il a, dans l'histoire, des titres d'ancienneté multiples. Jamais objet de tabou religieux, à la différence de certains produits tels que le vin, le sel apparaît comme le contraire même de la corruption. Sa dignité historique vient aussi de ce qu'il a joué, souvent, un role économique et politique; on a pu ainsi lui appliquer, par opposition au rôle actuel du pétrole, le surnom d'or blanc. Par son universalité enfin, il semble que le sel puisse être considéré comme un réactif sociologique et historique de premier ordre* (Mollat 1968: 12).[4]

General though these remarks are, they encapsulate much of what is of interest about salt: its common and "noble" uses, its varying sources, and its value in religious and social affairs.

Salt is used in many processes. While it is best known as a condiment and a preservative for foodstuffs, it is today used in the alkali trade (for the production of caustic soda and other sodium salts), the glass and soap industries, as a flux in metallurgy, as a fertilizer and insecticide in agriculture, as a reagent in glazing bricks, in dyeing and bleaching, in cement production, in the pharmaceutical industry, and in various other industries (Borchert & Muir 1964, 8; Sherlock 1921, 1). In the UK and other western countries at the present day, 30% of salt is produced as rock salt, mainly for de-icing roads; the rest is brine salt, used in industry (British Geological Survey 2006). Salt for human consumption represents a tiny amount of what is produced.

---

4   "Without making play of the paradox, salt is at the same time both a common and a noble product. Common, because it is exploited throughout the world, in all forms and all possible ways: sea salt by solar evaporation, rock salt extracted from mines, salt from springs by boiling and concentration, salt from ashes by boiling, salt resulting from the leaching (*lessivage*) of certain soils; these types of salt have always been used for human consumption and have become an almost unique preservation process over the centuries. Salt is noble because of its value for life, its indispensible character for every human being; in this respect, it is considered the real symbol of strength, like a purifying and regenerative principle. We may recall the evangelist's expression "salt of the earth". Sought out throughout antiquity, in history there are many indications of its long service. Never the object of religious tabous, unlike certain products such as wine, salt appears the real opposite of decay. Its historical worth also arises from the fact that it has often played an economic and political role; so it has been possible to apply to it the nickname "white gold", in contrast to the present-day role of oil. Lastly, because of its universal character, it seems salt can be considered a first-rate sociological and historical reagent."

Fig. 1.1. Salt for presentation to visitors (village museum, Oleksandrivka, Ukraine; photo: Author)

Ethnographically, it is known that salt is very commonly used to preserve meat and cheese products, as an antibacterial substance used to combat infection in wounds (in humans or animals), for treating a range of ailments such as rheumatism and arthritis, and in various rituals. In this we may recall the many remedies for animal ailments involving salt that the Roman writer Columella gave in Books VI-VIII of his *De re rustica*, written in the mid-first century AD. The greeting of visitors in peasant societies with bread and salt (*khlyab i sol*) (Fig. 1.1), and its variants in the different Slavic languages) reflects the important role played by these two items: bread as the "staff of life" (the basic foodstuff), and salt as the symbol of well-being.

It is a commonplace that humans and animals need a certain intake of salt to maintain health. Unfortunately there appears to be little agreement on what the requisite amount is, with widely differing figures appearing in the literature.[5] Kurlansky remarks: "Modern scientists argue about how much salt an adult needs to be healthy. Estimates range from two-thirds of a pound to more than seven pounds each year" (Kurlansky 2002: 9). Multhauf (1978: 2-3) points out the discrepancies in how much salt different authorities say is required; he settles on 4.5 kg per annum per capita for culinary requirements and national self-sufficiency in culinary salt. The topic has also been addressed by a number of other

---

5   The Salt Institute (in the US) likewise indicates a wide range of values: http://www.saltinstitute. org/Issues-in-focus/Food-salt-health/Human-salt-requirements (accessed 18 August 2013).

Author	Adult human	Horse	Cow
Nenquin (1961: 140)	12-15	50	100
Bergier (1982: 11)	5-6	50	90
Adshead (1992)	6-12		
Saile (2000)	1-10	10-50	15-90
Monah (2002: 137)	2-5		25 + 2 per l of milk
Cappuccio/Capewell (2010)	1.5		
Jockenhövel (2012: 239-40)	5-10		30-50
Golovinsky (2012: 338)	3-6 (min.) 16-20 (max.)		

Table 1: Required daily intake of salt (g) according to various authorities

authors, though archaeologists naturally have to rely on information provided by biochemists and biologists (e.g. Chapman & Gaydarska 2003). Recent studies by medical biologists have argued that the amounts usually quoted are greatly in excess of what is actually required (Cappuccio & Capewell 2010).

These differences are striking, and even allowing for the fact that they may reflect the difference between what is biologically necessary and what is actually consumed, when multiplied up they represent a huge potential discrepancy in calculations of what historical production might have required. The difference between the highest and the lowest is a factor of ten!

This has major implications for the salt requirements of groups of people, large or small, such as cohabit in farmsteads, hamlets, villages, towns and cities. More than one scholar has modelled the effects of such figures. Albrecht Jockenhövel (2012: 240), for instance, suggests that a Bronze Age settlement of about 75 persons would need 150-300 kg of salt per annum; 20 cows would need 220-365 kg; whereas one estimate for the output of the Hallstatt mines is only 2000 kg per annum. Chapman and Gaydarska did a similar exercise for the Tripolye "mega-sites" (Chapman & Gaydarska 2003), pointing out that potentially tens of thousands of kilos of salt were needed even for single sites, let alone whole regions. Clearly there are major discrepancies between what was apparently required, and what was allegedly available, that have to be overcome.

The point is, however, that people need salt, at least in some measure. Those who do not have any on their territory, in whatever form, need to obtain access to supplies. This simple fact has profound implications for human groups, now and – more especially – in the past.

The action of salt in the body

Sodium chloride (common salt) acts in the body through the ions of sodium and chlorine, which diffuse through the cell walls by osmosis. Sodium ions are positively charged, while chloride is a negatively charged ion of chlorine (through the addition of one electron). Together these are responsible for regulating the fluid balance in the bodies of living creatures. The human body is reckoned to

	Sodium	Potassium
Lean meat	80	400
Cow's liver	80	200
Chicken	100	460
Eggs	150	150
Shellfish	100	320
Goat's milk	80	140
Cow's milk	90	150
Wheat flakes	60	330
Potatoes	20	530
Cabbage	30	460
Plums	10	250
Oranges	4	450
Hazelnuts	20	600
Redcurrants	1	100

Table 2: Sodium and potassium content of some common foodstuffs (mg per 100 g). (Source: Walter 1986, 69)

contain about 0.4% sodium chloride, which means that a person weighing 50 kg would have some 200 g of common salt in solution in the body – a surprisingly large amount if one imagines it as dry salt.[6] Since the normal secretions of the body mean that this is constantly being lost, it has to be replaced.

Sodium is the element which has the biggest effect on health, in the sense that sodium deficiency is responsible for a range of ailments in mammals, actual or potential. Table 2 illustrates the sodium content of various common foodstuffs.

In a prehistoric context not all the foodstuffs listed in Table 2 would apply, of course (we can ignore potatoes and oranges, and, for periods before the Iron Age chickens as well), but other foods were available to supply the needs of these minerals. Given what we know about diet from plant and animal remains surviving in archaeological contexts of the Neolithic, Bronze and Iron Ages, balancing the diet in order to get sufficient intake of sodium and potassium should not have been a problem – except that for meat to contain these amounts, the animals themselves would have needed sufficient in their fodder.

The fullest and most systematic analysis of the effects of salt, or rather the lack of it, on the system, and a discussion of why humans and animals like the taste of salt, was provided by the eminent Australian animal physiologist and behavioural scientist Derek Denton. This work covered a great many topics that are not

---

6   http://sciencefocus.com/qa/how-much-salt-human-body, accessed 18 August 2013.

discussed in the archaeological literature, including the results of observation of and experimentation with animals.[7]

The availability of sodium is a crucial aspect considered by Denton. Given its "paramount role in animal metabolism", its availability in different environments becomes a crucial issue. Near coasts it is abundant; the further from the sea one travels, the less sodium rainwater contains, and consequently the less plants will receive – unless salt is present for other reasons. Particularly for successful reproduction, mammals "require quite large amounts of sodium for the tissues of the developing young and for milk during the nursing period". The study showed how depriving sheep of sodium has notable effects, among which is a "hunger for salt" in order to redress the balance (Denton 1984: chapters 9, 11, 12 etc).

The desire of animals for salt is abundantly demonstrated. Not only do sheep have a great appetite for salt, but many other herbivores do the same: reindeer like to drink human urine (supposedly for its salt content); deer of various kinds seek out salty pools or rocks – so much so that it is customary for hunters in various parts of the world to use the presence of such salt sources to lure animals. On the other hand, carnivores, while needing salt no less than herbivores, can get most or all of the sodium they need from the meat of the animals they eat.

History of research

Salt has long been recognised as an important element in the resources available to past peoples, and therefore an object of archaeological interest. Nenquin (1961, chapter 1) gave a full account of the early years of discovery, which need only be mentioned in brief outline here. His account was largely concerned with the 19th and early 20th centuries; for later periods he presented the material in conjunction with individual sites themselves.

While the technology involved in salt production can be taken back to (among other sources) Georgius Agricola's *De re metallica* in the 16th century (1556) (Fig. 1.2), studies of salt as such began in earnest in the 19th century. Early studies were those of Hehn (Hehn n.d. [1873]) and Schleiden (Schleiden 1875), both of whom devoted much space to the etymology of salt place-names, to classical and medieval references to salt, and to the presence of salt production areas in various parts of Europe and beyond. Schleiden in particular attempted to give specific detail about salt sources in Europe, including the most recent estimates of salt production in different countries – and arriving at a total for Europe of 75,633,121 *Zentner*,[8] the largest producers being Russia, Germany, France and England. Figures for the Carpathian region, including Wieliczka, are given as 3,356,666 *Zentner* – a surprisingly small total given the huge production already taking place at Wieliczka alone, to say nothing of Bochnia in Little Poland, the Transylvanian

---

7   Denton's studies on sheep and other animals, involving withdrawal of salt, sometimes including surgery, might well fall foul of ethical approval nowadays, at least within the European Union. Since the Department of Archaeology at Exeter University runs a Masters in Experimental Archaeology, I have idly wondered from time to time whether controlled experiments withholding salt from students might be carried out – naturally in return for a reduction in fees!

8   A *Zentner* is a sack of salt weighing 50 kg, so this total is about 3.8 million tonnes.

A—Wooden dipper. B—Cask. C—Tub. D—Master. E—Youth. F—Wife.
G—Wooden spade. H—Boards. I—Baskets. K—Hoe. L—Rake. M—Straw.
N—Bowl. O—Bucket contains the blood. P—Tankard which contains beer.

Fig. 1.2. Georgius Agricola: salt boiling in the early modern period (De re metallica, 1556)

and Maramureş sources (such as Ocna Dej, Ocna Mureş, Praid, Ocna Şugatag, Solotvino etc). A sign of the times is Schleiden's remark about Turkey:[9] "There are many other countries to which nature has denied the gift of salt, or whose people – as in Turkey – are too lazy to exploit the salt available to them"; and "European Turkey possesses the largest salt deposits on its territory, but the people there are too lazy to exploit them and import salt from neighbouring countries just for their most essential needs" (Schleiden 1875: 177-8).[10]

With the discovery and excavation of the Hallstatt cemetery in the 19th century, it was quickly realised that the richness of the graves might be explained by the fact that Hallstatt was also the site of a major salt source and that control of the salt sources could have led to a centre of wealth developing at Hallstatt. Although prehistoric materials were being found in graves from the 1840s under J.G. Ramsauer, the significance of the salt mine was first brought to wide attention by F. von Hochstetter (1881), following which articles by J. Szombathy (1900), M. Much (1902) and others added to the known corpus of information.

Meanwhile attention had been drawn to the sites around Halle, specifically the unusual pottery (which we now know to be briquetage) (Schmidt 1894), and in Lorraine. In France, it was particularly the Seille valley that attracted early attention: finds in the region of Marsal and Moyenvic were the first, being noted as long ago as 1740 by Félix-François Le Royer d'Artezet de la Sauvagère, and repeatedly mentioned in the 19th century. Among the many authors cited by Nenquin, the work of A. Schliz and A. Voss deserves mention (Schliz 1903; Voss 1901). Work in the Halle region really took off in the 1950s, however, with the contributions by Karl Riehm (Riehm 1954; 1961; 1962) and later Waldemar Matthias (Matthias 1961; 1976); and in the Seille valley in the 1970s with the work of Jean-Paul Bertaux (Bertaux 1976; 1977). Later work in both areas has elucidated many of the problems that these authors highlighted (see the relevant chapters below). Iron Age material was found in the late 19th century at La Panne near Bray on the coast at the French-Belgian border.

Other early work in Austria and Germany included that at Bad Nauheim in Hesse and Bad Reichenhall in Bavaria; these and other sites became much better known in the 20th century, as discussed below.

In Britain, the Red Hills of the east coast were first noted and studied in the 1870s, though there were earlier indications of interest in them. H. Stopes (1879) published a short study of the "salting mounds" of Essex and by the turn of the century a Red Hills Exploration Committee had been set up. The work of R.A. Smith laid to rest any doubts about the function of these sites and the ceramics found on them (Smith 1918); since that time more and more sites of this kind have

---

9   "Turkey" in this context refers to the Ottoman Empire, and Schleiden may have had Bulgaria and
    Wallachia in mind, or perhaps Bosnia (Tuzla).

10 „Es gibt aber auch immer noch viele Länder, denen die Natur die Gabe des Salzes versagt hat oder in
    denen die Bevölkerung wie in der Türkei zu faul ist, das bei ihnen vorkommende Salz auszubeuten"
    (p. 178); "Die europäische Türkei besitzt die grössten Salzlager im Lande, das verkommene Volk ist
    aber zu faul, sie auszubeuten und führt nur für den allernothdürftigsten Bedarf der Menschen Salz
    von den Nachbarländern ein" (p. 177).

been found on and near the East coast of England, with most work taking place in East Anglia and Lincolnshire (see below).

In Poland, the great mines of Wieliczka and Bochnia were exploited intensively during the Austrian period, but archaeological research dates mainly to the post-WWII period. Early records are mentioned by Hehn and Schleiden, but this did not lead to archaeological work. The inter-war period saw some interest in the salt sources of east Galicia, but not to investigations of their archaeological potential.

In 1943 a volume of the Ciba journal was devoted to salt. Here a brief account of salt in ancient times was given by J. Schroeter, briefly discussing the classical sources, depictions in Agricola, and the Hallstatt and Hallein mines as they were known at the time, with briefer mentions of other Iron Age sites in Germany and France (Schroeter 1943).

The great historian of technology R.J. Forbes devoted a chapter in his third volume to salt (Forbes 1955); this concentrated particularly on the ancient sources, in all parts of the ancient world, and on the processes of brine-boiling. Forbes had little first-hand knowledge of the archaeological material, however.

Salt archaeology came of age with the publication in 1961 of the first systematic study, *Salt: a study in economic prehistory*, by Jacques Nenquin (1925-2003). Nenquin's overview covered the whole of Europe and the whole of prehistory, down to Roman times. He considered the ancient and medieval written sources as well as the full range of archaeological material evidence, the technologies and the dating, and concluded with a discussion of the economic importance of salt and its appearance in toponymy and mythology. With this work, the archaeological study of salt – over a wide canvas and not just in individual sites or countries – was established. All subsequent authors have had to build on Nenquin's work.

Since then, we effectively enter the modern period of salt study. The publications by Riehm and Matthias in Halle, and Jodłowski in Wieliczka, shed important new light on sites and areas that were by then well-known. One of the first conferences devoted specifically to the study of salt was that held in Colchester in 1974 (de Brisay & Evans 1975). The proceedings are subtitled "The study of an ancient industry", and the participants included leading salt scholars from continental Europe (P.L. Gouletquer, M. Tessier, A Jodłowski) as well as numerous British researchers, mainly those interested in salt in eastern England and the Midlands, but also including contributions on a global scale. Here for the first time salt was considered as a world-wide commodity, not just something restricted to Europe or even particular areas of Europe.

An account of the history and distribution of salines (salt evaporation sites), with especial reference to Germany (and above all eastern Germany) was given by Emons and Walter (1988). The account of the evaporation methods used in medieval and modern salines is highly detailed, and returned to in the relevant chapters below.

Conclusion

Salt archaeology has become an established subject of study over the last 150 years. From early investigations in France, Germany, Austria and Britain the topic is now a matter of interest to many scholars across Europe and beyond. The biology of salt is well understood, even if opinions differ about its true effect on the human body and how much is needed to maintain health. Historically, people have sought out salt, sometimes in huge quantities; archaeologically this may be less easy to detect but the production and movement of salt is not in doubt. As the following chapters will discuss, sites of different kinds and periods across Europe are providing new information on the technology and date of ancient salt production. Salt has long been known to be important in ancient economies and societies; the scene is now set for us to find out *how* important.

Chapter 2

Salt: what it is, where and why it appears

What is salt?

Salt is an "evaporite", a geological term that covers a large variety of minerals that may be called "salts" in a general sense. Evaporites are water-soluble mineral sediments that result from the concentration and crystallization by evaporation of water-based solutions. These may be chlorides, such as halite (NaCl, sodium chloride, common salt), sulphates, such as anhydrite ($CaSO_4$) or gypsum ($CaSO_4.2H_2O$), or carbonates such as calcite ($CaCO_3$). A less common type of evaporite is represented by the "potash salts", i.e. those containing potassium, such as sylvite (KCl, a naturally occurring form of potassium chloride).

Rock-salt, or halite, consists of the mineral sodium chloride with a small admixture of impurities (magnesium, sulphur, calcium). The pure mineral sodium chloride contains 60.6% chlorine and 39.4% sodium (Sherlock 1921).

A detailed account of the composition of seawater-derived salt deposits was provided by Braitsch (1971). Since these salts are produced by evaporation, one can use experimental evaporation to see how the evaporites actually form (Borchert & Muir 1964, 74 ff.). Thus in a 100 m evaporite succession, seawater will produce a thickness of 78 m of halite, with 9.4 m of magnesium chloride (bischofite), 5.7 m of magnesium sulphide and 3.6 m of calcium sulphide (gypsum/anhydrite), whereas the Zechstein evaporites produce the same amount of halite but 16 m of gypsum and negligible quantities of the other minerals

Table salt as available in shops today is usually iodized, i.e. it has iodine, in iodide or iodate form, added for health reasons. In its natural form it is not free-running like salt from our salt-cellars, which also has an anti-caking agent added. Ancient salt was not like this; instead, it would have been similar to other sorts of salt that are available today at a higher price. Rock salt can be bought, with no additives and completely unprocessed except for coarse grinding; in this case only the purest deposits are appropriate for table use, while less pure deposits are suitable for animals, for anti-icing on roads, or for industrial purposes. Sea salt, such as the famous Sel de Guérande collected from the salt marshes near the Atlantic coasts of France (Fig. 2.1), is also available unprocessed; such salt is much more concentrated than processed table salt. These last two forms of salt give a much better idea of how the substance would have appeared to the ancients.

Today's world production of salt is around 180 million tonnes (Emons & Walter 1988, 5), one third of which comes from the sea and most of the rest from mining.

Fig. 2.1. Sal de Guérande: sea salt production in western France (photo: Maxironwas, Dreamstime.com)

Origin and occurrence of salt deposits

Salt deposits in the form found and exploited today are the result of tectonic activity.[11] The salt itself typically arises from the one-time presence of ancient seas, the changes taking place over geological timescales (salt-bearing formations in Europe typically being of Miocene age, between 23 and 5 million years ago). These changes result principally from the pressure of overlying sediments onto salt strata, causing deformation and the upward thrusting of the deposits. If the amount of tectonic compression is small, the deposits may merely be folded and the stratigraphic sequence preserved. Where it is greater, the salt may be pushed upwards in the fault zone, and depending on the local situation, the dome may form a conical shape, a cylinder, or an inverted cone – a dome or diapir (overview in Braunstein & O'Brien 1968). In Europe, such domes or diapirs are common in northern Germany, Spain and Romania. Where the diapirs approach the earth's surface, they may outcrop and be quarried or mined on the surface, or rainwater percolating down to them may rise up in the form of brine springs – a clear indication that salt is present and potentially recoverable – though in the Carpathian zone brine springs can also merge from relic seawater preserved underground.

---

11   How and why salt deposits form is a matter that has been presented in the literature many times. Excellent overviews are available from a number of sources Alsop *et al.* 1996; Braitsch 1971; Jenyon 1986.

The so-called Badenian salinity crisis, dated to a period starting at around 13.8 million years ago (De Leeuw *et al.* 2010), was responsible for the deposition of massive evaporite deposits in the central European Paratethys Sea. A range of geological formations are present from central and eastern Europe containing the salt that is the subject of much of what is discussed in this book (convenient summary in Bukowski 2013). For south-east Poland and Ukraine, Ślączka and Oszczypko (2002) provide a detailed account of the geological conditions that led to the development of salt formations.

In terms of salt occurrence, the most important geological element in north and north-west Europe is the Zechstein formation, a unit of sedimentary rocks laid down in the European Permian basin that stretches from eastern England to northern Poland. Most of the salt from central and northern Germany belongs to this group. The salt of the northern calcareous Alps, or *Haselgebirge*, is of Upper Permian age and results from extreme tectonic deformation. The rock is in fact a "two-component tectonite" consisting of rock salt and mudrock.

In southern Europe, salt deposits are found widely across Spain, with rock salt occurring predominantly in the Keuper formations of the Triassic succession that are biased towards the north (Cantabria, Basque provinces) and east (Pyrenees, Iberian ranges, Betic Cordillera) of the country. Salt domes, or diapirs, are concentrated in the Cantabric trough, though they are also present in Andalusia and the Betic chains. The recovery of sodium salts from Neogene strata of the Madrid basin using brine springs and wells has a long history with those at Carabaña, for example, exploited in Roman times. Potassium salts are found in the Ebro Basin, which extended across southern France and northeast Spain during the Eocene era, but silvinite – a mixture of potassium chloride and sodium chloride – is also known from sedimentary geologies in Navarra (García del Cura *et al.* 1996; Lunar *et al.* 2002: 492; Rios 1968).

To the north, in France, the rich salt deposits are concentrated in the east and south-west of the country, the latter corresponding to the Eocene-Oligocene and Triassic strata of the Aquitaine Basin in Aquitaine and Midi-Pyrénées, counterpart to the Ebro Basin to the south of the Pyrenees in Spain. Other Eocene and Oligocene-era sedimentary geologies bearing important salt reserves, particularly potassium salt, are found in Alsace, in a discrete zone to the north of Mulhouse, between the Rhine and the Vosges Mountains. Elsewhere in France most salt is found in Triassic-era formations, notably in the Paris Basin, 100-300km west of the city, in the Jura Mountains of Franche-Comté, and around Montpelier in Languedoc-Roussillon (Bérest *et al.* 2005; Gale 1920).

In Britain, the Permian-era Zechstein formation that extends at depth between Teesside and Lincolnshire in the east of England is of less importance in terms of the recovery of salt than the Triassic Mercia Mudstones (formerly called Keuper marls) that are concentrated within the Cheshire Basin and north Shropshire, but that are also known in Lancashire, Somerset, Dorset, and Worcestershire. None of the salt occurrences in Britain is found on the surface, owing to dissolution, with extraction via natural brine springs, mining/drilling and pumping, solution mining, and room and pillar mining (British Geological Survey 2006).

The composition of British rock salts was given long ago by Sherlock and others. Thus Cheshire rock-salt varies between 99 and 78% sodium chloride, with magnesium chloride and calcium sulphate being present along with an amount of insoluble material (marl) (Sherlock 1921, 8), this latter making up even larger quantities in very impure rock-salt.

Ireland has little salt, but a significant source of rock salt lies at Kilroot, Co. Antrim.

Seawater and brine

The concentration of salt in seawater varies from sea to sea, but typically lies in the range 3.1 to 3.5% (the Red Sea is exceptional at 4%, while the Black Sea contains only 1.8-1.85%).[12] This means that one litre ($\approx$ 1 kg) of seawater contains around 31-35 g of dissolved salts (most but not all sodium chloride). These figures indicate the surprising amount of water that has to be boiled off in order to end up with the salts it contains.

Brine springs vary considerably in their salt content, even from day to day depending on rainfall, strength of the sun, as well as the depth of the salt massif across which the spring flows. Emons and Walter give figures for brine sources in eastern Germany: 0.79% for Lindenau, 0.96 for Schmalkalden, 6.40 for Salzungen springs, but 25.70% for bored sources at Salzungen from 1842 (Emons & Walter 1988, 21) – a remarkable difference which shows the filtering effect of the soil materials between the solid salt and the surface. Walter (1986, 69) and Emons & Walter (1988, 20) give further figures: Kołobrzeg (Poland) 5.5%, Werl: 8%, Solivar (Slovakia) *ca* 10%, Frankenhausen 12%, Stassfurt 17%, Halle (Saale) around 20%, Lüneburg 24.7%, Hallstatt 25%. One assumes that where people had a choice, they went for those springs with the highest concentration.

Simon (Simon 1995: 46) gives figures for various salterns in Germany, ranging from 1% at Wimpfen to 20-25% at Lüneburg, with Halle/Saale at 18-22% and Schwäbisch Hall at up to 5%.

Salt lakes appear in various parts of the world. While the Dead Sea may be the most famous in the Old World, with a salinity of 33.7% (approximately 337 g of dissolved salt per litre of water), the great Salt Lake of Anatolia (Tuz Gölü) (Fig. 2.2), with salinity up to 32.9%, is equally important for an understanding of how salt might have supplied prehistoric settlements in the region (Erdoğu *et al.* 2003). Other well-known salt seas include the Caspian and Aral Seas, though the former's salinity at 1.2% is too low for effective exploitation while the latter's has gone sky-high with attendant environmental problems. Lake Baskunchak in Astrakhan oblast, Russia, is a much more likely source of ancient exploitation. In the New World, the most famous example may be the Great Salt Lake in Utah, but there are

---

12 The official scale in use is the Practical Salinity Scale, or PPS, which measures salt in ‰ rather than %. Figures are given here in % as this is generally easier to understand. PSS is in fact defined as the conductivity ratio of a sea water sample to a standard KCl solution, so there no exact equivalence between salinity and salt content.

Fig. 2.2. The Great Salt Lake (Tuz Gölü) in Anatolia (photo: Author)

Fig. 2.3. Rock salt outcrop at Bisoca, Romania (photo: Author)

many others, such as the Zuni salt lake in New Mexico – a sanctuary for the local Native Americans to the present day (Duff *et al.* 2008: 9).

All these brine sources (other than those mentioned as exceptions) are potentially exploitable by evaporation, either solar or artificial.

Richness of salt sources

In Europe today, the largest producer of salt is Germany, with 17.44 million tonnes in 2011; this is divided between rock salt (8.77 mt), brine salt (2.2 mt) and "salt-in-brine" (6.46 mt).[13] The Netherlands, Britain, France and Ukraine all produced 6-7 mt in 2011, Poland and Spain around 4.4 mt. Romania was once a large producer but is now less important, having declined from over 5.3 mt in 1988 to 2.25 mt in 2011 (Brown *et al.* 2013; Lofty *et al.* 1994).

From the point of ancient production, with only a couple of exceptions (Hallstatt and Hallein) deep mines are irrelevant; only where they led to the emergence of brine on the earth's surface would they have had any significance. As discussed below in Chapter 3, where rock salt outcropped, it could have been quarried; deep mining seems only to have come into being in the Roman period.

As will become clear, many parts of continental Europe were exploited for brine; on the other hand, relatively few were demonstrably used for rock extraction – most famously Hallstatt and the Dürrnberg at Hallein, but the huge salt massifs in the Carpathian zone (Fig. 2.3) must have served as ready sources of rock salt, then as now.

In other words, any search for the "richest" salt sources is actually a search for the richest archaeological evidence of exploitation. There must have been major sources that were not exploited, and there were relatively minor sources that were intensively exploited. From today's perspective, it is hard to separate the two.

Conclusion

Europe has abundant salt resources, in various forms. From the perspective of the ancient economies, many – though not all – areas had access to salt in one form or another. It is this access to salt that I shall now explore period by period.

---

13   Salt-in-brine: brine supplied to industry for use in the electrochemical process for the production of chlorine and caustic soda (sodium hydroxide), and in the Ammonia-Soda process for the production of soda ash (British Geological Survey 2006).

Chapter 3

Production techniques through the ages

Producing salt is not a simple matter. Even though the sources of salt are all around us, in the form of seas, rocks and springs, extracting the salt from its parent body requires dedicated equipment, time, and manpower. Only in those situations where the sun's heat acts on salt water to produce salt crystals that can be picked up and used without further processing was the procedure straightforward, requiring little input of energy.

Nowadays table salt is refined and iodized (iodine being added for health reasons). It is possible to obtain unrefined salt in areas of the world where simple technologies are used, but people in westernized societies do not usually make use of this possibility and have no idea of what pre-industrial salt would taste like, raw or cooked. The sea salt that one can buy in the shops may be refined to a greater or lesser extent, and may not even come from the sea but from salt marshes. Modern rock salt likewise has been processed using modern technologies for grinding and removing impurities.

As recently as 1999, one author could write: "What is not known from the excavation reports published in this volume… is exactly how the salt was made… The information from Bronze Age, Iron Age and Roman salterns is scant… Many theories and hypotheses have been put forward; some are more convincing than others" (B.B. Simmons in Bell *et al.* 1999).

In considering the range of techniques that are, or have been, in use for salt production prior to the industrial period, it is necessary to consider a range of sources. However, apart from archaeological materials (which constitute the main source utilised in this book), the most useful sources are the Greek and Roman authors in the classical period (which have the advantage of having been written at the time the ancient saltworks were in use), and ethnography, which may be well understood but can only serve as an analogy. Unfortunately many of them are rather unspecific as to technological process, so they may be supplemented by medieval or modern sources, such as the treatise by the sixteenth century German scholar Georgius Agricola, *De re metallica* (1556; English translation H.C and L.H. Hoover, London 1912). Book XII deals specifically with salt production, and includes detailed accounts of how to make salt from seawater in pits, pans or cauldrons, with details of furnaces. The writings of Agricola, however, should really be regarded as a kind of ethnographic parallel, since there is no certainty that any or all of the techniques described and illustrated might apply to the prehistoric period.

The techniques

Burning of halophyte plants

A commonly used technique known from ethnographic studies, and attested indirectly from plant remains on archaeological sites, is that of burning halophyte plants (for instance common glasswort (*Salicornia europaea*), found on many European salt springs, or the sea grasses found on tidal saltmarshes), and washing the ashes to obtain salt. This method is also that to which Aristotle apparently alludes (below), and was the basis of a flourishing salt trade on the continental part of the North Sea coast in medieval times.

Evaporation of salt water

Salt water is either that in the sea, or that emerging on land from underground salt deposits, or in salty streams or rivers, or in sands and muds. Seawater typically contains 3.5 % dissolved salts, mostly the ions of sodium and chlorine, but it is mixed with other minerals and impurities, notably magnesium and calcium, as well as algae and sediment. Evaporating seawater either through insolation (typically in salt lagoons), or by the application of fire, produces salt crystals, but without further processing these are bitter and unpleasant to the taste. Usually, therefore, fresh water needs to be added and the process repeated. The evaporation of inland brine may not suffer from these problems, depending on its composition; simply collecting it in containers and boiling it slowly for a lengthy period may be enough. Calculations have been made on how long brine evaporation might take by various methods (Akridge 2008), but given the number of variables and unknowns, applying these to the situation in prehistoric Europe seems fraught with difficulty.

A related technique is that of gathering salty sand or mud, filtering it by some means (typically by putting it in a pit and allowing the solids to settle), drawing off the brine and evaporating it as above (described by, among others, Hocquet 1986: 8 ff.).

Lagoons and salt marshes

Coastal salt lagoons were evidently the main means of production in Etruscan and Roman Italy; the coast north of Ostia was one of the main areas used, but many parts of the Italian peninsula must have also served the purpose. It is easy to see such lagoons in many places today around the Mediterranean (Fig. 3.1); in most cases there is no specific archaeological evidence for ancient production, however. The collecting of salt crystals in salt marshes, typically just inland from the sea, is also common; this is what one finds along French Atlantic coasts (the sel de Guérande, for instance).

Fig. 3.1. Salt lagoon on Kos, Greece (photo: Christopher Smart)

Fig. 3.2. Seawater evaporating in a coastal saltworks on Malta
(photo: Viktorfischer, Dreamstime.com)

Salting yards

Modern coastal production where no lagoons are present can also take place in what are best described as salting yards, where a hard surface, often of concrete, is used for seawater to evaporate (Fig. 3.2). The example shown would best function in the summer when the heat of the sun was strong enough to burn off the water and leave the salt crystals.

Briquetage

Sites where sea water was evaporated using briquetage are especially common in France, eastern Britain and the coastal parts of the Low Countries. Many parts of the west coast of France and the east coast of Britain have such evaporation sites; in Britain these are well known under the title Red Hills, as typically found in the form of large heaps of burnt and broken ceramic in Kent, East Anglia, Lincolnshire, and further north (Fig. 3.3). Something very similar occurs in other parts of the world, for instance the Basin of Mexico (Santley 2004).

Brine from inland sources was also evaporated using briquetage, and here for quantity and range of material, and recent studies of high quality, there is no rival to France, where numerous sites in Lorraine have been excavated and detailed study of techniques carried out (excellent summarising account in Daire 2003). I discuss the prehistoric briquetage sites in detail in the following chapters, period by period.

Other containers

A full discussion of techniques used since the Middle Ages in central Europe is provided by a number of authors, including H.-H. Emons and H.-H. Walter (1988). A range of equipment was used to concentrate brine, usually involving large iron pans which could be placed on a fire or hearth. Lead pans were also used, certainly in the medieval and early modern periods (as Agricola tells us), and very probably also in antiquity as a precursor to iron pans (photo in Carpentier *et al.* 2012: 169).

The use of such pans for boiling and evaporating brine has been widespread since early modern times. Numerous examples can be seen in museums in salt-producing districts and are known from ethnographic research (e.g. Oleksandrivka and Drohobych Museum, Ukraine: Figs. 3.4, 3.5) (Romanian examples from Cavruc & Chiricescu 2006). Essentially the use of these pans is a variant of the briquetage technique, involving the application of heat to containers holding brine; the advantage is that the pans can be used again and again, unlike briquetage which was used once only.

The graduation tower (*Gradierwerk*)

A technique that became common in Europe (especially Germany) in the last 300 years of production, prior to modern industrialisation, was that of the *Gradierwerk* ("grading device" or graduation tower, Polish *tężnia solankowa*) (Fig. 3.6). This

Fig. 3.3. Reconstruction of salt evaporation in progress on a Red Hill in Essex (© Essex County Council)

Fig. 3.4. Salting pan in Oleksandrivka church, Ukraine (photo: Author)

Fig. 3.5. Salting pan in Drohobych museum (photo: Author)

consists of a high wall or shed, constructed by means of a wooden framework, containing organic materials like straw or thorn branches, down which the brine trickles, the principle being that exposure to the wind and sun is prolonged and evaporation thus made more effective, with a minimum of technical equipment or expense – the only constraint being the energy required to raise the brine to the top of the shed. Such walls could be 10 m high and hundreds of metres long; the largest in Europe is at Ciechocinek in Poland. Other modern examples are at Inowrocław in the Kujawy district of Wielkopolska (Great Poland) (Fig. 3.7), at Bad Salzuflen, Bad Dürkheim, and elsewhere in Germany. The exposure to the air and wind helps evaporate some of the water in the brine, thus concentrating it; and by repeating the process, a considerable increase in salt concentration can be achieved.[14] The water has to be pumped up to the top of the tower, but otherwise little man-made energy is required.

Earlier versions of this construction used bundles of straw for the purpose; in Germany this became common after around 1570. Straw was not very effective, however, and introduced impurities which reduced the quality of the salt; as a result by the 18th century it was replaced by blackthorn (*Prunus spinosa*), which did not deteriorate in the same way, and being hard, springy and thorny, could be used in quite thick bundles. The drops of brine were segregated more finely, and heavy metals would concentrate in calcium deposits on the thorn branches, rather than continue into the concentrated brine. A further advantage was that these and other

---

14   Figures for the saline at Kösen on the Saale in Sachsen-Anhalt in 1839 show this effect (Emons & Walter 1988: 26; figures rounded up):

% NaCl in brine	1st grading	2nd grading	3rd grading	4th grading
2.7	8.5	13.2	19.9	24.8

Fig. 3.6. The graduation tower at Inowrocław (photo: Author)

Fig. 3.7. Detail of the graduation tower at Inowrocław (photo: Author)

impurities would form as hard deposits of calcium carbonate, and would thus be removed from the resulting concentrated brine.

While it is not possible to demonstrate the existence of such devices in prehistory, it is easy to imagine that this simple but effective technology, or a variant of it, was used to raise the concentration of salt in brine springs prior to further processing. Indeed, the techniques suggested in the interpretation of the Romanian production sites (see below) are variants on the theme of increasing the exposure of brine to the elements, in order to promote the evaporation of water and concentration of salt. Whatever the real method of using the wooden troughs in the Carpathian Basin turns out to be (pp. 63-6), the possibility that brine dripped through the holes onto a textile or similar surface, and that the resulting salt crystals were picked off, remains plausible.

Mining and quarrying

Rock salt varies considerably in composition; in theory any rock salt could be ground into a powder and used unmodified, but in practice only the purest would be considered sufficiently appetising to be used on its own for human consumption. Either rock salt or sea salt might be added unrefined to cooked food, however, since the taste of the food would mask that of the salt.

Where salt outcrops on the earth's surface, it is mined, either by means of deep mines (shafts and adits) or by surface extraction – where the dug material does not go down deeper than a few metres. Nowadays most salt is mined, and mining is what is known from major sources, such as Wieliczka, in recent centuries. In Roman times, too, it appears that deep mining for salt took place in various parts of Europe, for instance in Romania, just as mining for metal ores is known from many parts of the Roman world, while the East Alps saw such processes at work in the Iron Age (Hallstatt and the Dürrnberg). Earlier than that it is uncertain whether mining, as opposed to surface quarrying, took place. It cannot be ruled out, however, that mining occurred in the Bronze Age, since it is certain that deep mining for copper ore was taking place, just as deep mining for flint occurred in the Neolithic.

The quarrying of rock salt appearing on or near the surface was probably carried out in conjunction with other techniques, such as the use of troughs and fences in Romania (below), or evaporation techniques using underground salt ponds, as seen in medieval Hallstatt.

Troughs and fences

The technique involving wooden troughs, in combination with wattle fences and other wooden installations, has been known about in outline for many years, but only in recent times has it become more fully understood as a result of fieldwork in Romania (Chintăuan 2005; Harding 2009; Harding & Kavruk 2010; 2013). I consider the technology involved in this technique (or collection of techniques) in detail below (Chapter 5). In essence, it involves hollowed out tree-trunks, perforated with multiple holes in the base, the holes plugged with pegs that were themselves perforated. The intention seems to have been to allow water to drip slowly onto an exposed rock salt surface, forming depressions which could be enlarged into cracks that enabled chunks of hard rock to be broken off; there are other possibilities too, considered below. This technique was accompanied by the construction of numerous fences forming roundish or oval enclosures; these were probably places where brine could be stored in order to increase its concentration by insolation. The fact that these fences were not watertight seems not to have mattered; presumably they would have acted as a sufficient barrier to the ingress of fresh water and the egress of salt water to have served their purpose sufficiently.

Ethnography

Salt is an important commodity at the present day in non-industrialised communities. Although many of them nowadays use commercially produced salt, which is cheap and readily available, there are still many situations in the world, and indeed some in Europe, where people stick to the old traditions: they collect brine or mine rock salt, and use the material for traditional purposes. In recent years, a number of studies have been conducted to examine these technologies and uses, both world-wide and in peasant societies in Europe. It is worth mentioning them here because they may shed light on techniques that may have been present in antiquity, though this cannot of course be guaranteed.

Romania

Ethnoarchaeological studies on salt production have been particularly popular in Romania, where in both Moldavia and Transylvania there is a burgeoning literature. Among the first such pieces of work was a study by Alexianu and colleagues on Moldavia, since elaborated a number of times (Alexianu *et al.* 1992; Alexianu & Weller 2007; Alexianu *et al.* 2007; 2008); for Transylvania the work of Cavruc's team, and especially that of Andrea Chiricescu (Deák) is important (Chiricescu 2013; Deák 2008). In both provinces it is mostly brine collection rather than any other form of production that is involved (Figs. 3.8 – 3.9), but peasant quarrying of surface outcrops was observed by Deák at Dumitra near Bistrița, and by Cavruc and me in Muntenia at the "Muntele de sare" (salt mountain) at Bisoca in Buzău county (Fig. 2.3).

Cavruc and his team have made exhaustive investigations of the equipment used for the manipulation of brine and other salt products in Transylvania, including a study of variations between different ethnic groups (Romanian, Hungarian, and Roma) (Cavruc & Chiricescu 2006).

New Guinea

Discussion of New Guinea salt owes much to a classic paper by Godelier (1969). He described how salt cakes were made by specialists, over five to six days, using a tunnel-shaped oven with 12-15 moulds, 80 cm long and 12 cm wide, arranged above it, each mould containing a small tub of impermeable banana leaves, the top

Fig. 3.8. Peasant collecting large quantities of brine from the well at Lunca-Poiana Slatinei, Moldavia (Romania) (photo: Author)

Fig. 3.9. Peasant collecting brine from a spring at Drajna de Jos, Prahova, Romania (photo: Author)

kept open so that brine could be poured in. After the slow boiling process finished, very hard salt cakes 60 to 72 cm long and 10 to 13 cm were obtained, weighing 25-30 kg. These were trimmed carefully to shape and wrapped in dry banana leaves to keep them dry; they were now ready for transportation and exchange.

An account by Pétrequin and colleagues (Pétrequin *et al.* 2000; 2001) describes how in New Guinea particular plants are soaked in brine and then burned, the salt crystals being picked from the ash and compressed into packets or cakes wrapped in plant material. Something similar was described by Agricola (*De re metallica* XII, 556 in the Hoover translation). These cakes were then exchanged over long distances, serving not only as a means of transporting an important physiological supplement but also forming part of a social regulatory system where salt could assist in marriage alliances and matters of war and peace.

Other areas

Filtration troughs, made of clay mixed with rice straw or grass, and burnt to make them hard, were used in Thailand, salty sand being collected up and placed in the troughs with water being poured on (Nitta 1997). A spout at the bottom of the trough led the water off into pots; the soil was collected up and dumped and the brine boiled. This process is attested ethnographically and seems to correspond to installations found in excavation, associated with prehistoric pottery.

In Mexico, one ethnographic study has described the "tapeite process", in which the salty crust is collected from saltwater marshes and placed in a large filter (*tapeite*) made of wood or cane slats covered with palm or grass, and with adobe sides (Good 1995). Brackish water is poured over the earth, and the liquid seeps through the filter into a holding tank. It is then put in drying pans of plastered mud to evaporate in the sun, the pans being refilled twice a day and the earth being removed. The salt crystals are collected each evening and placed in a plastered area to dry off. A related technique in an inland area also used the filtration technique, though the precise details differ (Williams 1999). Archaeologically speaking, it is clear that few remains of these processes would survive; the numerous mounds covered in sherds that have been recorded in parts of Mexico may well represent a version of the Red Hills known from eastern England, and reflect comparable technological processes.

A somewhat different technique, though still involving the filtration of soil saturated with salt, was described by historical writers in Guatemala and with variations observed in recent times (Reina & Monaghan 1981). Here fine soil was spread over hot mineral water taken from water-holes; it would then be collected up into baskets, and water poured over it, the concentrated brine being collected in pottery containers below, and then boiled.

A variant on this technique is also recorded in Uganda (Connah 1991), one difference being that the earth used for salt impregnation is used over and over again. Filtering water through plant ash rich in salt is another well-attested technique.

In Botswana, as in many other places, salt is collected from the surface of salt pans from the end of winter to the start of summer (Matshetshe 2001).

Much information has been obtained about salt production in Niger, thanks to fieldwork by a French team (Gouletquer 1975; Gouletquer & Kleinmann 1984). Several methods are used: the gathering up and filtering of salty earth, solar evaporation, filtering and boiling salt, and salt making from plant ash. Most detail was provided on a technique which involves a combination of filtering and briquetage: salty earth is gathered up into basketwork filters and washed, the brine being collected underneath; a kiln is built, with clay containers supported on pedestals; brine is poured in, and the evaporation process started. Once it had gone on for 24 hours, and the kiln had cooled down, the containers were broken up and the salt cakes this formed entered the distribution network.

Written sources: classical antiquity, medieval and early modern

The story of salt in classical antiquity is a somewhat varied one. It is generally agreed that salt was regarded as of high importance to all the peoples of antiquity, which makes it all the more frustrating that so little is said in the ancient sources about its production and movement. The Latin word *salarium* (salary) is thought to derive from money allowed for salt, coming to mean the total number of allowances in money and kind that Roman officers required; over time this came to cover the reimbursement of expenses for magistrates and senators; Pliny the Elder also refers to control of the *via Salaria*, linking Ostia with the Sabine lands, as an important element in the rise of early Rome. In the famous passage of Pliny quoted below, salt is equated with good appetite, good health and wit: "a civilised life is impossible without salt" (see also Appendix).

In spite of this evident importance, Pliny apart, mentions of salt are invariably brief and need a considerable amount of interpretation in order to get a real picture of how and where salt was produced, and how it reached those areas where there was none. Fortunately a comprehensive account has recently been published, which removes the need to compile and assess all the ancient sources (Carusi 2008); this amplifies earlier work that considered the importance of salt in the Roman economy (Giovannini 1985) (this author is also responsible for the informative entry in *Der Neue Pauly* (English translation *Brill's New Pauly*, vol. 12, 2008, 902-5).

Pliny's account

The most informative passage about salt and salt production in all the ancient texts is a long section in Pliny's *Natural History* (Book XXXI, 70-92), which is cited *in extenso* in the Appendix. The technical aspects of this account have been considered in detail by Healy (1999), as well as by many other authors (e.g. Forbes 1955). It is thought by some scholars that much of Pliny's account is derived from the Hellenistic philosopher Theophrastus, who wrote a treatise *On Salts, Soda and Alum* (lost), as well as his celebrated work *On Stones*. Another source is believed to have been the 1st century BC Roman writer M. Terentius Varro, though his surviving corpus does not include more than mentions of salt in farming and food production processes.

The most important statements in Pliny relating to production are these (all translations by A.D. Godley, Loeb edition, 1921; the paragraph numbers are mine):

1. All salt is artificial or native; each is formed in several ways, but there are two agencies, condensation or drying up of water. It is dried out of the Tarentine lake by summer sun, when the whole pool turns into salt, although it is always shallow, never exceeding knee height, likewise in Sicily from a lake, called Cocanicus, and from another near Gela. Of these the edges only dry up; in Phrygia, Cappadocia, and at Aspendus [Greek colony in Pamphylia; all these areas are in Anatolia], the evaporation is wider, in fact right to the centre. There is yet another wonderful thing about it: the same amount is restored during the night as is taken away during the day. All salt from pools is fine powder, and not in blocks. Another kind produced from sea water spontaneously is foam left on the edge of the shore and on rocks. All this is condensation from drift, and that found on rocks has the sharper taste…

2. At Citium in Cyprus and around Memphis salt is taken out of a lake and then dried in the sun…

3. There are also mountains of natural salt, such as Oromenus in India, where it is cut out like blocks of stone from a quarry… It is also dug out of the earth in Cappadocia, being evidently formed by condensation of moisture. Here indeed it is split into sheets like mica; the blocks are very heavy… At Gerra, a town of Arabia, the walls and houses are made of blocks of salt cemented with water… the region of Cyrenaica too is famous for Hammoniac salt, itself so called because it is found under the sand. It is in colour like the alum called *schiston*, consisting of long opaque slabs

4. Of artificial salt there are various kinds. The usual one, and the most plentiful, is made in salt pools by running into them sea water not without streams of fresh water, but rain helps very much, and above all much <warm> sunshine, without which it does not dry out…

5. It is also however made in Crete without fresh water by letting the sea flow into the pools, and around Egypt by the sea itself, which penetrates the soil, soaked as I believe it is, by the Nile. Salt is also made by pouring water from wells into salt pools…

6. In Chaonia [in Epirus, north-western Greece] there is a spring, from which they boil water, and on cooling obtain a salt that is insipid and not white…

7. In the provinces of Gaul and Germany they pour salt water on burning logs. In one part of the provinces of Spain they draw the brine from wells and call it *muria*…

8. King Ancus Marcius gave a largess to the people of 6,000 bushels of salt, and was the first to construct salt pools.

For this last, compare Livy (History I. XXXIII. 9): in the reign of Ancus Martius (AUC 114-138, 640-616 BC) "the Maesian Forest was taken from the Veientines, extending Roman domination to the sea, and at the mouth of the Tiber the city of Ostia was founded, with salt-works created nearby".[15]

Other authors

Herodotus in describing the peoples and places of North Africa has a lengthy presentation of the northern edge of the Sahara, i.e. inland "Libya" (IV. 181-5). He refers to a series of "masses of great lumps of salt in hillocks", with springs of sweet water rising from them. The "peoples that dwell on the ridge as far as the Atlantes" have a mine of salt on it [the ridge] every ten days' journey, and men dwell there. Their houses are all built of the blocks of salt" (Loeb edition 1921, trans. A.D. Godley)

Aristotle, *Meteorologica* II, iii. 359a.25 – b.4, after explaining about salt solutions, and the properties of the Dead Sea, says this:

> *"In Chaonia there is a spring of brackish water which flows into a neighbouring river that is sweet but contains no fish... For they boil off some water from it and let the rest stand; and when it has cooled and the moisture has evaporated with the heat salt is left, not in lumps but in a loose powder like snow. It is also rather weaker than other salt and more of it must be used for seasoning, nor is it quite so white. Something of a similar sort happens also in Umbria. There is a place there where reeds and rushes grow: these they burn and throw their ashes into water and boil it till there is only a little left, and this when allowed to cool produces quite a quantity of salt"* (Loeb edition, 1952, trans. H.D.P. Lee).

In seeking to understand the importance of these passages for our knowledge of prehistoric and early salt production, a number of matters stand out. It is clear from Pliny's account, along with the briefer quotes from other authors, that salt was obtained either by evaporation or by mining; the former being much commoner in the Mediterranean environment with which Pliny was most familiar. Most, like the passage from Aristotle, refer to the evaporation of salt water, whether sea water or brine from springs. Paragraph 3 refers to the mining of salt, which is stated to occur in Oromenus in India, Cappadocia,[16] Cyrenaica and Hither Spain. The reference to Cyrenaica is perhaps supported by the quote from Herodotus. Paragraph 7 refers to the evaporation of salt by throwing brine onto burning timbers or leaves, and using the resulting ash as a source of salt; this, and the collection of salt crystals from a brushwood fire, is, as mentioned above, attested ethnographically at the present day. The technique described by Aristotle is somewhat different: halophyte plants are burned, the ashes put into water, and the water evaporated until the crystals could be picked off.

---

15 Silva Maesia Veientibus adempta usque ad mare imperium prolatum et in ore Tibere Ostia urbs condita, salinae circa factae.

16 Columella refers to Cappadocian rock salt in his discussion of treatment of ailments of the eyes of oxen (*De re rustica* VI, xvii, 7).

What is less satisfactory about these passages, and especially about Pliny's account, is that little idea is given of the relative importance of the different sources, in terms of both quality and quantity. He also gives no real indication of how the mining of salt was carried out, though we may be fairly sure that deep mining for salt did indeed occur in the Roman period, certainly in Dacia, as it did for metals both there and in other provinces of the empire (Wollmann 1996).

Salt was evidently an important concern in ancient Mesopotamia, with a number of different varieties being recorded; the area has many sources, of various kinds, most of which were exploited and listed in Ottoman sources. Understanding the ancient texts to shed light on production methods in antiquity, however, is far from easy (Potts 1984).

Conclusion

Various sources of evidence give us a picture of how salt is and has been produced in pre-industrial societies. Even modern techniques sometimes have information of value to us, since the physical processes to be undertaken are the same. It is, however, ironic that in some instances we have a better understanding of the technology of prehistoric societies than we do of classical ones; Pliny, after all, was not writing an economic history and obviously did not consider it important to cover certain aspects about which we would dearly like to know more. Nevertheless, armed with this information, we are now in a position to consider the production of salt period by period.

Chapter 4

From earliest times to the Chalcolithic

Introduction

Since salt is desirable for human health and as an additive to food, and always has been, one may presume that from earliest times people – like animals – will have sought out salt sources or foods that contain some salt to use for the purpose. The extent to which hunter-gatherer groups specifically seek salt is not clear, but there is ethnographic evidence that they at least seek to know where salt-rich muds and plants are to be found. Much of the available ethnographic literature on the subject relates to modern peoples whose subsistence is only partly based on hunting and gathering (for instance the New Guinea studies of Pétrequin and colleagues: Pétrequin *et al.* 2001).

For the Palaeolithic there is no evidence for an interest in salt other than the proximity of sites to salt sources, though no clear connection has been established (this would require a full analysis of site and source location, which has not been carried out). A cluster of sites in close proximity to a major salt source, with few or none further away, might be indicative. One might presume that the exploitation of brine springs, rock salt or salt lagoons might be adventitious, in other words, people made use of them when they were present but did not otherwise seek them out (it is unlikely that seawater would have been used in food, since it is bitter and full of impurities, though it could have served a purpose as a preservative). Since up until the Upper Palaeolithic meat is presumed to have been the main food source, it is likely that enough salt was ingested naturally for there to have been no need for supplements, especially if the animals being hunted had access to salt-rich vegetation. With the increase in the gathering of plant foods in the Upper Palaeolithic, the situation may have changed somewhat. Plants growing in salty areas might have been specifically sought out.

For Nenquin in 1961, little was certain about exploitation prior to the Bronze Age. His map and tables (Nenquin 1961: 127 ff., Map I) only list Hallein and Hallstatt in Austria, and Oued Beth in Morocco, as having certain Neolithic evidence, though it is unclear on what he based this assessment. Otherwise a series of "possible" sites in Germany, Britain and France is listed; in most cases more recent assessments have not supported the claims. Saile's work (2000: 150 ff.) again only suggests Neolithic production at a minority of sites across Europe, with briquetage in the Wieliczka area and Halle-Giebichenstein the only certain cases. In other respects it is merely proximity of Neolithic sites to salt sources that comes into question, for instance the large number of Linearbandkeramik sites in the Schwäbisch Hall area, or finds in the Werl area in Westphalia. Pottery interpreted as briquetage occurs in Late Neolithic and Corded Ware sites, including burials, but this was not regarded by Saile as conclusive. In 2002 Weller gave an outline of the situation, listing those sites where he considered salt production was more or less assured (Weller 2002a). More recently Saile has made a study of potential Neolithic salt production in central Europe (Saile 2012), reiterating the slight evidence for certain production prior to the Lengyel period in Poland or the Late Neolithic sites around Halle.

In fact, the first certain evidence for salt production in Europe does come from the Neolithic. It has been suggested that one can infer a Mesolithic interest in salt-producing areas. The only putative Mesolithic evidence comes from Provence, where the bottom of a salt well at Moriez (Alpes de Haute Provence) produced pieces of pine, one of them worked, that are interpreted as having formed a small enclosure for brine evaporation. Two of these gave radiocarbon dates of 6845 ± 65 (5791-5663 cal BC at 68.2% probability, 5877-5630 at 95.4%) and 6745 ± 45 BP (5706-5625 cal BC at 68.2% and 5726-5567 at 95.4%), dates which would fall in the late Mesolithic of the area (Morin 2002; Morin *et al.* 2006).

The site at Lunca-Poiana Slatinei (Tîrgu Neamţ, Moldavia, eastern Romania), where a small tell lying immediately next to a salt well has produced Criş culture pottery, has been much trumpeted as the earliest salt production site in the world (Weller & Dumitroaia 2005; Weller *et al.* 2008b; 2009) (Fig. 4.1). The ten radiocarbon dates (on charcoal) fall in the range 7100 ± 40 BP to 6590 ± 50 BP (6052-5899 to 5618-5479 cal BC at 95% probability). Unfortunately the publications do not give the exact location of the samples in relation to the cultural layers, so it is not known if they fell in stratigraphical order, but the general picture is clear.[17] The oldest and youngest dates barely overlap with any others at 1σ, so it would be wise to consider the calibrated range as falling between about 5900 and 5600 cal BC.

Criş pottery was also recovered at the salt springs at Solca-Slatina Mare (Suceava), also in Moldavia, without radiocarbon dates (Ursulescu 1977) (Fig. 4.2), and Cacica (Suceava) (Fig. 4.3). The latter, however, is said to be accompanied by Cucuteni pottery – in other words a millennium later (Andronic 1989). At present it is possible to see briquetage in considerable quantities on the surface at both sites (Fig. 4.4).

In the Balkans, few places show direct evidence of salt production. Circumstantial evidence comes from the presence of Starčevo sites near salt sources in Bosnia, at Gornja Tuzla for example (Tasić 2000: 36; 2002). Tasić even suggests that the number of different cultural groups in south-eastern Europe in the Neolithic indicates a free-for-all as far as salt is concerned, "a common interest in the important commodity [bringing] different groups of people together" (Tasić 2000:

---

17   Fig. 5 in the 2009 publication shows four stratigraphical locations described as being the source of the ten dated samples, but neither the text nor the diagram of dates (Fig. 4) specifies where each sample comes from – they are simply arranged in chronological order.

Fig. 4.1. The tell beside a brine well at Lunca-Poiana Slatinei (photo: Author)

Fig. 4.2. Neolithic pottery spread in the brine stream below a brine well at Solca-Slatina Mare, Suceava, Romania (photo: Author)

Fig. 4.3. The mine at Cacica (Suceava, Romania). Briquetage is eroding out of the bank on the right (photo: Author)

Fig. 4.4. Briquetage found with Neolithic pottery at Cacica (photo: V. Kavruk)

40); also that the richer a site was in terms of material culture, the more likely it was to be connected to the salt trade. I return to these matters in Chapter 9.

Vinča-period exploitation of the rock salt at Tuzla in Bosnia is claimed on the basis of briquetage-like pottery from the town (Benac 1978); the distribution of Impressed Ware sites in Dalmatia has been said to relate to that of modern salt evaporation sites (Gaydarska 2003: 111); and the proximity of the Varna cemetery to the Black Sea and to Provadia (see below) is also regarded as suggestive. Gaydarska also points to the proximity of tell sites to salt sources in eastern Bulgaria (Gaydarska 2003: 117-9); the tell at Mirovo (Provadia) inland from Varna is the obvious example (see below). The identification of salt springs and salt lagoons by Gaydarska and Chapman (2007) has provided much useful information for further field survey, but no definite association with sites.

Much the most important source for salt production in the Neolithic and Chalcolithic periods in the Balkans is Provadia-Solnitsata, 40 km inland from the Black Sea coast at Varna (Figs 4.5-4.6). Here, extensive excavations since 2005 by Vassil Nikolov near the modern saltworks have uncovered extensive settlement material and a great deal of salt-related pottery and on-site installations (Nikolov 2008; 2009; 2010; 2012). Provadia lies over the Mirovo salt diapir. The site and associated salt production fall into a number of phases. According to the excavator, the first occupation of the tell falls in the Karanovo III-IV phase and dates around 5500 cal BC, when salt was evaporated using thin-walled bowls made specially for purpose, and placed in dome-shaped ovens. A large building contained one of these ovens, quadrangular in shape and not unlike normal bread ovens; such constructions were present over a large part of the tell. In the following phase, pit installations were created 150 m from the tell near the Provadia river; these were found to be full of ashy material, sherds and daub. The pots were of a somewhat different form in this period.

For the Carpathian Basin proper (i.e. inside the Carpathian ring), there is no specific evidence for Neolithic salt exploitation, though discussion has taken place about its likelihood and its probable effects within the economy of the rich cultures of the Hungarian Plain (Bánffy 2013). Neolithic sites in Transylvania have been considered possibly to be linked with salt (Lazarovici & Lazarovici 2011). One such settlement is Gura Baciului near Cluj (Lazarovici & Maxim 1995). The site is located in the immediate vicinity of salt springs (Maxim 1999), and was inhabited for the whole of the Early Neolithic Criş culture, with broad contacts within the East Carpathian Early Neolithic (Lazarovici & Maxim 1995: 346-352). Kalicz has suggested that salt may have played a crucial role within these contacts, with Méhtelek communities playing a part in the salt trade (Kalicz 2011; 2012: 121). Within the Körös culture, a certain funnel-shaped, coarse pottery type is sometimes assumed to have been used for evaporating brine (Fries-Knoblach 2001: Taf. 6/1).[18]

---

18   I am grateful to Eszter Bánffy for these references.

Fig. 4.5. The Neolithic and Chalcolithic site at Provadia-Solnitsata (photo: Author)

Fig. 4.6. Part of the Chalcolithic salt-processing area at Provadia, showing large quantities of sherds in the section (photo: Author)

Claims that one or another site represents the oldest salt mining in the world have been made for more than one place. Hard on the heels of that relating to the Lunca site came another, concerning salt mining at the Duzdaği mine[19] in Azerbaijan (Marro 2011; Marro *et al.* 2010); the brief accounts published so far indicate a date in the second half of the fifth millennium BC (based on the Late Chalcolithic Chaff-Faced Ware present in part of the site: Marro 2010). At this site, although the artefacts indicated activity at this early date, the main period of exploitation came a millennium later, in the mid-fourth millennium BC. Whether Duzdaği is really earlier than Lunca remains to be seen; from what is published so far the dates from the latter are earlier, but radiocarbon dates have not yet been obtained at Duzdaği; the dating is based solely on the pottery.[20]

The Cacica site in Moldavia must be approximately contemporary with the little understood pottery of Lengyel date, said to be briquetage, from Barycz and other sites in the Wieliczka area of Little Poland (Fraś 2001; Jodłowski 1971; 1977). Here the classic Lengyel culture material is represented by large numbers of sites, containing hearths and similar installations evidently connected with brine evaporation, as well as pottery interpreted as briquetage. Fraś (2001: 305-319) has listed 438 sites in the Wieliczka area with Neolithic material, the majority only known from surface material but a small number excavated. These cover all phases of the late Neolithic Lengyel, the post-Lengyel Malice culture, the Baden (Radial Pottery) culture, and TRB; the largest number of sites with diagnostic sherds belong to the classic Lengyel, with smaller numbers from subsequent periods. While it remains unclear why there should be this concentration on Lengyel, with many fewer sites before and after, the sheer number, along with the characteristic features on site and the pottery, suggests that salt production experienced a *floruit* during these centuries. Much remains to be elucidated, however, about exactly how production worked in this area and period.

Few illustrations of these sites have been published; that at Barycz site VII (Kraków) is usually cited (Bukowski 1985: 46-7 Fig. 8; Grabowska 1967; Jodłowski 1968; 1971: 111 Fig. 24). Here a series of slight ditches was present, two of them apparently leading in to roughly square pits with sides of 2 m or 1.8 m (interpreted as settling tanks), with hearths and a large wooden construction also present. The process was interpreted as follows: brine was led into the tanks and left for some time for impurities to sink to the bottom. It was then put into broad-necked vessels and boiled over open fires. The resulting crystals were packed into pointed-base pots and left to dry in the ashes of the fire; a salt cake made in this way would weigh 700-1000 g, and could be taken out and moved in exchange without further manipulation.

At Provadia, it was in the subsequent Middle Chalcolithic period, assigned to 4700-4200 cal BC and thus contemporary at least in part with the Varna cemetery, that the major development of salt production took place. This area, partly overlying installations of the preceding phase, covered more than 0.5 ha

---

19 Duzdaği: "salt mountain" (duz = tuz, salt).
20 I am grateful to Catherine Marro (Lyon) for information about the dating of the site.

and contained at least five large saltmaking installations. These were again large pits, filled with huge quantities of sherd material. Typical for this phase are large open tub or bucket-like vessels, with rusticated surface and flat base; these come in three sizes (Weller 2012: 71-3 Figs 5-6). These were apparently packed into the bottom of the pits, wood added and lit, and the whole thing allowed to boil and then cool, so that brine was turned into crystals in conical cake form; the pot would then be smashed and the cake retrieved. This phase of production has been seen as industrial in scale by the excavator; huge quantities of sherds are present, and ceramic ladles were found, probably to stir the brine. The vessels could contain between 1 and 80 litres of brine, theoretically producing somewhere between 1.1 and 170 kg of salt cake (depending on vessel size and crystal density) (Weller 2012: 80-81 Fig. 16).

Salt production was only one part of what went on at Provadia; settlement on the tell was surrounded by a defensive rampart and palisade, constructed in several phases; there were pits on the site containing deposits of inverted pots, antlers, querns, and other paraphernalia; and there were human burials in some of the pits, with a formal cemetery to the south-west.

Some questions remain about aspects of salt production at Provadia, for instance the use of the thin-walled Late Neolithic vessels as potential briquetage; one would imagine that they would crack under the heat of fire applied directly to them, so they might merely have been used for drying crystals in the presence of gentle heat. But for the Chalcolithic it is impossible to imagine that the vast quantities of sherd debris in pits with clear indications of fire can have served any other purpose. Provadia is without question the most important pre-Bronze Age salt production site in Europe. One may ask why production there did not continue into later centuries; perhaps the progress of excavation and survey will produce more finds to answer the question.

The other area where there is good evidence for Neolithic – probably 5th and 4th Millennium BC - salt production is Catalonia. The *Muntanya de Sal* (Salt Mountain) at Cardona (Fig. 4.7) is one of the most impressive salt massifs visible on the surface in western Europe. Still exploited until 1990, it is now a significant tourist attraction for the region – adding to the magnificent castle and medieval streets and buildings of the town.

Investigation of the salt archaeology of the area has been particularly intensive in the last twelve years (Figuls *et al.* 2007; Figuls *et al.* 2013; Weller 2002b; Weller & Figuls 2007).[21] While no actual prehistoric working site survives, the extensive presence of ground stone tools in the valley leading from the outcrop, many showing signs of battering that can only have come from quarrying activities, seems indisputable evidence of Neolithic working. Remarkably, these tools are in hard stones not available locally; they were brought to Cardona from the mountains near the coast or the Pyrenean foothills, presumably because their hardness would be appropriate for striking against the hard rock salt. Analysis of sites and finds in

---

21   I am grateful to Alfons Figuls and colleagues for conducting me round the site and showing me other evidence of Neolithic exploitation in the area.

Fig. 4.7. The Muntanya de Sal, Cardona, Catalonia (photo: Author)

this part of Catalonia indicates a likely date in the local Middle Neolithic, whose radiocarbon dates indicate a range 4500-3500 cal BC. This was also the period when the famous variscite mines at Gavà (south-west of Barcelona) were being exploited, its products moving widely through northern Spain and France; a strong case has thus been made for extensive trading networks in the Catalan Neolithic, salt being one of the major traded commodities.

Salt up to the end of the Chalcolithic: conclusions

It will be evident from the foregoing that direct evidence of Neolithic salt production is scanty, and restricted to a few well-investigated sites in the eastern half of Europe; in the west, the evidence is proxy in nature. Before the Neolithic, there is no direct evidence of any sort; any presumption of salt production has to rest on the proximity of sites to salt sources. The same is true for much of Europe in the Neolithic, but finds in Romania and Bulgaria show an early exploitation, probably initially on a small scale. The Lengyel material in the Wieliczka area presumably dates to the mid fifth millennium. With the Chalcolithic period at Provadia (mid fifth millennium BC), things took on a quite different complexion: the scale of production was much larger and the technology more advanced. Production at Cardona then took off in the centuries around 4000 cal BC.

A final word may be interposed concerning the "earliest" salt production in Europe, or the world. Here it is necessary to remember that there is a difference between salt *mining* and brine *evaporation*. As discussed above, production at Lunca appears to have taken place in the sixth millennium cal BC, but this was almost certainly by evaporation. The Karanovo III-IV phase at Provadia would be more or less contemporary with Lunca, again using evaporation. The first mining may well be that at Duzdaği in Azerbaijan in the fifth millennium, though radiocarbon dates are really needed. It is of course likely that where salt rock appears on the earth's surface, people will have quarried it from very early times; here the evidence of site proximity to salt sources may be relevant. Nevertheless, we await the discovery of Palaeolithic or Mesolithic sites with direct evidence for salt production.

Chapter 5

The Bronze Age

The change from a stone age to a metal age was notable for many features other than purely economic and artefactual. While in recent years our understanding of Neolithic economy and society has developed in sophistication and scale, the sequence of events that followed in the later third and more especially the second millennium BC was of a different order from what went before. In artefactual terms the arrival of metal-using in a big way marked a major transformation in what was available to the artisan and to the population more widely, even if some items were restricted to certain groups in society. Metal production was only the most obvious development; other major changes can be observed in burial practice and in social and political organisation, as settlement form and distribution demonstrate. In the series of technological developments which we can discern (for instance in nautical technology), salt production is one which shows both continuity and innovation from the preceding period.

One of the very few finds of actual salt comes from the Bronze Age: it is recorded from the Ourania cave in eastern Crete (Kopaka & Chaniotakis 2003). Half a kilo of salt was recovered during excavation of the site, both large and small pieces (including powdered salt), apparently found in or with broken pottery containers. This find appears to be unique, even if the presence of salt might be detectable by analysis of residues as suggested by these authors, citing J. Evans). The only other example is that of small pieces of rock salt found in the excavation of a site probably of Lausitz culture date at Pobiednik Wielki 15 km east of Kraków (Reyman 1934: 39 ff.).[22]

Bronze Age salt production was, with a few notable exceptions, rather poorly known until quite recently. Although there were some finds of Bronze Age briquetage from France, central and southern Germany, and Britain, it was really the sites around Halle (Saale) in Sachsen-Anhalt that provided the only sizeable corpus of material (see below), while knowledge of Bronze Age salt-mining at Hallstatt was restricted to one area of shafts and a few early radiocarbon dates. Speculative articles had been written about the situation in Poland (Bukowski 1963) and Romania (Rusu 1963; 1981), mainly concerned with other artefact classes that might have indicated a salt connection. In other countries the situation remained quite vague, even though some scholars were well aware of the proximity of salt sources to major archaeological sites.

---

22 The finds came from Site 5 in the Luty field, but the field produced Neolithic and Iron Age material as well as Lausitz.

The enormous increase in interest in and research on prehistoric salt production over the last 20 years has changed the landscape completely. As a consequence, much more is now known about Bronze Age production than previously, though it remains true that the situation across Europe is patchy – depending partly on the survival of evidence, and partly on the interest taken in it by local scholars, who may or may not have conducted searches for relevant evidence.

Four types of production can be identified in the Bronze Age in Europe, two involving the evaporation of salt water (brine or sea water), using briquetage and the application of heat, or by means of insolation, the action of the sun, on salt water in lagoons; one involving the mining or quarrying of rock salt; and one involving a mixture of mining and concentrating brine, using the "trough technique" (see below). While all these had been suggested in previous decades, it is only now that the true picture is becoming clear.

Briquetage

Briquetage is usually considered to be one of the main hallmarks of ancient salt production, especially for the Iron Age and Roman periods though also, as we have seen, in Neolithic contexts. In Bronze Age contexts, however, it is much less frequently found than in later periods; and while in some areas a considerable range of forms is known, in others our information comes from a very small number of vessels or other forms, such that we cannot tell exactly how it operated in the overall process of evaporating brine and transporting the resulting salt crystals.

Germany

Much the largest quantity of Bronze Age briquetage in Europe comes from Germany, and specifically from the area in and around Halle (Saale) (Fig. 5.1). These finds have been much studied over the years. Originally recorded in the 19th century, the work of Riehm, Matthias and others have shown the range of forms known and the archaeological contexts from which the briquetage comes (Matthias 1961; 1976; Riehm 1954; 1961; 1962). More recently the work of Müller and others has extended the area of interest to neighbouring districts, such as Erdeborn (Müller 1987; 1988; 1996), Hitzacker or Brehna (von Rauchhaupt & Schunke 2010). Exploitation of Bronze Age date might have taken place at a number of other sites, for instance Bad Reichenhall (Bavaria). Bad Nauheim, Bad Mergentheim, Bad Frankenhausen, Lüneburg, Bad Bevensen and several other places (all listed and referenced by Saile 2000: 154-160, Abb. 5) – though in most instances the evidence is uncertain or circumstantial, and no briquetage has actually been found. On the other hand, isolated finds of briquetage come from several Lausitz culture graves in Saxony and Brandenburg (Bönisch 1993; Petzel 1987; von Rauchhaupt & Schunke 2010), presumably indicating production nearby (and arguably a special status for the saltworker – see chapter 9). Jockenhövel has listed more grave sites in central and eastern Germany from which small pieces of briquetage have been recovered (Jockenhövel 2012: 246-9), as well as a comparison with graves in the same area that contain smithing material.

Fig. 5.1. Early Bronze Age briquetage from Uichteritz (Ldkr Weißenfels) and Lützkendorf (Ldkr. Merseburg-Querfurt) (photo Juraj Lipták, © Landesamt für Denkmalpflege und Archäologie Sachsen-Anhalt)

Poland

Briquetage of Neolithic date has long been known from Wieliczka, as was discussed above, but later briquetage has been found only more recently. The largest collections come from sites in the neighbourhood of Kraków, notably Bieżanów site 27 but also Kraków-Rżąka site 1 (Kadrow 2003; Kadrow & Nowak-Włodarczak 2003). These consist of large quantities of typical briquetage, mainly goblets with splaying foot (Fig. 5.2); other characteristic forms such as pedestals seem not to have been identified. Interestingly, these sites lie somewhat off the line of the salt massif that runs through this part of Little Poland, suggesting that brine, or semi-processed brine, was brought here from some kilometres distant.

France

While enormous quantities of briquetage are known from the famous Iron Age sites in the Seille valley in Lorraine (see below), the quantity of Bronze Age briquetage is much lower. Some sites in that area do indicate a Bronze Age presence (Bertaux 1976; 1977; Poncelet 1966), while in Brittany and elsewhere on the Atlantic coast there are also indications of pre-Iron Age workings (Giot *et al.* 1965; Gouletquer 1969; 1970; Tessier 1960), though more material dates to the Iron Age. A small amount of briquetage found in a double enclosure at Étaples-Mont Bagarre, in the Canche valley (Pas-de-Calais), was associated with Middle Bronze Age pottery

(Desfossés 2000: 114 Fig. 38.11; Marcigny & Le Goaziou 2012), though there were no specific indications of salt-working on this site (unlike the nearby Sorrus sites – see Chapter 6).

While no briquetage as such was recovered from the site, excavations at Salies-du-Salat (Haute Garonne) in south-west France produced a range of features, including four vats formed by water-tight clay-lined pits, a hearth, an arrangement of large numbers of sherds from big pottery vessels that may have formed a kind of container, and a pit filled with blocks of ophite with more sherds (Marcigny & Le Goaziou 2012). The pottery belongs to the Middle Bronze Age

Britain

Bronze Age briquetage has been known in Britain for at least 40 years, but it is only in the last decade that its extent has become clear. Nenquin (1961: 130-1) was only able to suggest a couple of sites with possible Bronze Age evidence, neither of them certain and neither confirmed by more recent study. One of the first to draw attention to the definite existence of briquetage on a Bronze Age site was David Gurney (1980) in his publication of material from a site at Northey near Peterborough. Other sites excavated in the 1970s that included briquetage were Mucking (Essex) (Bond 1988; Jones 1977), Fengate, Peterborough (Pryor 1980), Hullbridge, Essex (Wilkinson & Murphy 1986; Wilkinson & Murphy 1995) and Billingborough (Lincolnshire) (Chowne 1978; Chowne et al. 2001). Later work in the 1980s and 1990s provided more evidence, e.g. at Tetney (Palmer-Brown 1993).

At Brean Down the briquetage is associated with Middle Bronze Age contexts (J. Foster in Bell 1990: 165 ff.). The finds were made at the foot of a steep cliff just above the beach (Fig. 5.3), and consist of a standard range of pedestals and trays (Fig. 5.4). At Billingborough pits and hearths were found in Phase 2, belonging to the Late Bronze Age / Early Iron Age (radiocarbon dates cover a broad span of the first millennium cal BC), with substantial quantities of briquetage; although there was later activity it seems that the briquetage belongs to this phase (Cleal and Bacon in Chowne et al. 2001: 56 ff.); the site was considered the earliest in the area and among the earliest in the country (ibid. 92-3).

Most of the sites that have come to light in recent years include only small quantities of briquetage, certainly tiny by comparison with the huge amounts found in the later Red Hills. The question arises as to whether such sites were concerned with actual production, or rather with the distribution of salt in ceramic containers. Work by Janice Kinory has now shown that 31 sites of Bronze Age date have evidence for salt production or distribution, in the form of briquetage (Kinory 2012: 12-14, Fig. 4 Table 1). Some of these are well known, such as Mucking (Essex) or Brean Down (Somerset); others come from preliminary reports or the "grey" literature. Kinory (2012: 12) distinguishes between production and "non-production" sites: thirteen of the former, with on-site evidence in the form of hearths or similar installations for brine evaporation, and eighteen of the latter, consisting solely of briquetage. The distinction is not easy to make from the site

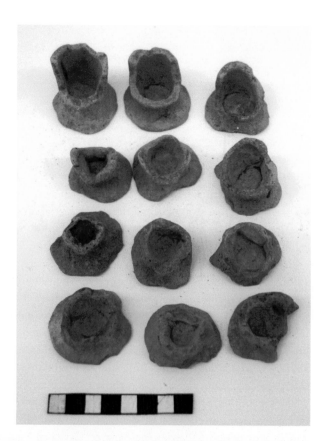

Fig. 5.2. Briquetage from Kraków-Bieżanow site 27 (photo: Author)

Fig. 5.3. Brean Down, Somerset, south-west England: view of the site from the south. The area from which the briquetage came is marked by the red arrow (photo: Author)

evidence, especially as production did not involve large-scale installations such as can be reconstructed from later sites of "Red Hill" type.

Spain and Portugal

A useful short summary of the situation in Iberia was published recently by Terán Manrique (2011), making a detailed discussion unnecessary. A short review has also been published by Nuria Morère (2002).

Several parts of Spain are rich in salt sources, and over recent years several of them have been the subject of detailed investigations. The Salt Mountain of Cardona I have considered in the previous chapter; there is no specific evidence for its Bronze Age exploitation, though a scatter of Bronze Age finds lie in its vicinity. Instead, the Iberian evidence comes mainly from inland and coastal salt lagoons, around which sites containing coarse ceramics assumed to be briquetage occurs. There is a notable concentration on the Beaker period, which is unusual in a European context; since this was a period when metallurgy saw a huge expansion in the Iberian peninsula one may perhaps connect the interest in salt with other technological – and social – developments at this time.

A number of sites in Iberia have been recognised as potential prehistoric salt production places. Typically these consist of areas of burnt soil or clay in the vicinity of salt springs or lagoons, and an abundance of pottery which might be interpreted as briquetage. These include Espartinas (Ciempozuelos, near Madrid), where areas of burning, interpreted as fires resulting from the evaporation of brine in large coarse pottery vessels, were accompanied by pottery of the Chalcolithic and Beaker period (Ayanagüena Sanz & Carnaval García 2005; Carvajal García et al. 2003; Valiente Cánovas & Ayanagüena Sanz 2005; Valiente Cánovas & Ramos 2009). At Las Marismillas (Seville) on the lower Guadalquivir, seventeen oval and oblong structures were interpreted as brine evaporation installations, with large quantities of fragmentary pottery, similar to the Espartinas forms, that was probably briquetage (Escacena Carrasco 1994; Escacena Carrasco et al. 1996; Escacena Carrasco & de Zuloaga Montesino 1988)

A perhaps typical site, recently investigated, is Fuente Camacho in Upper Andalusia (Terán Manrique & Morgado 2011). Although only one of many saltworks in the interior of Andalusia, it has recently attracted attention and undergone excavation because of the presence of prehistoric pottery near the modern working area. Lying on the Arroyo Salado, a secondary tributary of the river Genil west of Granada, the area has an area of modern production, one where "ethnographic" production took place (i.e. in historical times using simple technologies), and an area with large quantities of pottery lying close to salt springs. This pottery, the bulk of which belongs to the Copper and Bronze Ages, is associated with areas of burning and ashy layers in the exposed sections, attributed to the lighting of fires for the evaporation of brine.

At O Monte da Quinta (Benavente, Santarém, Portugal), areas interpreted as structures for brine evaporation ("possible combustion structures") consisted of elongated ditches associated with much pottery of Chalcolithic type, some of it regarded as potential briquetage (Valera et al. 2006).

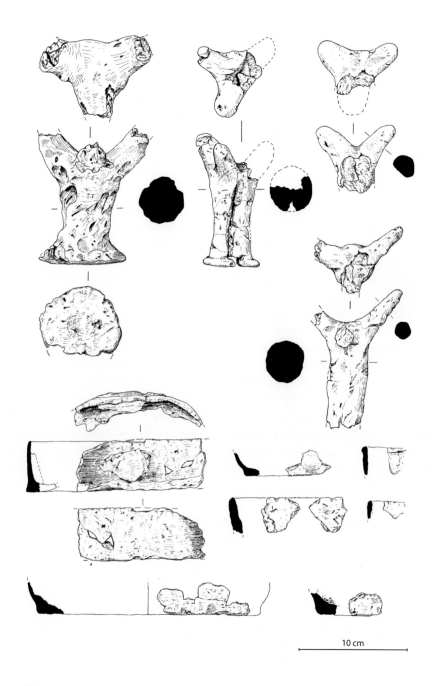

10 cm

Fig. 5.4. Brean Down, Somerset, south-west England: briquetage from the Middle Bronze Age levels (source: Bell 1990)

Villafáfila

The lagoons of Villafáfila form a Natural Reserve lying between Zamora and Benevente in Castilla y León province. The largest is represented by the Salina Grande, but there are many other lagoons in the area. Work by the University of Valladolid and Aratikos Arqueólogos in recent years has established that salt production began at least as early as the Chalcolithic (pre-Beaker) period (Abarquero Moras & Guerra Doce 2010; Abarquero Moras *et al.* 2010; Abarquero Moras *et al.* 2012; Guerra Doce *et al.* 2011). Since 2007 extensive survey work in the region has shown that of 55 archaeological sites registered, 36 are situated in the immediate environs of lagoons less than 1.5 to 2 km from their edges, and a further 19 a little further away. The majority are small, less than 3 ha in extent. Of those 55, 13 could be attributed to the pre-Beaker period, two to the Beaker period, 30 to the Early Bronze Age, five to the Final Bronze Age and four to the Iron Age. Several were prehistoric but could not be defined more closely, while one (Fuente de San Pedro) had possible Neolithic activity (a few had Roman or medieval occupation) (Abarquero Moras *et al.* 2012: 33 ff.).

The concentration on the Early Bronze Age is remarkable, as is the decline following that period, the reasons for which were the subject of speculation by the team and which remain unclear.

Geophysical prospection on a number of sites showed that hearths or burnt areas were widely present, and excavation at three sites in the area uncovered the remains of brine evaporation places, including pits filled with clay for filtering the brine, places for heating the brine with clay stands or plinths, and areas of clay burnt red, with ash and other remains of firing. At Molino Sanchon II a sequence of activity could be reconstructed, starting with a set of installations for heating and evaporating brine (Abarquero Moras *et al.* 2012: 143 ff.; Guerra Doce *et al.* 2011). After this, wells were dug, and then brine evaporation continued; finally, after a phase of waste dumping, pits for brine filtering using clay were dug, and further heating took place. A significant amount of the pottery here was decorated in Beaker styles; a small amount of what was identified as briquetage was present. Six radiocarbon dates fall between 2500 and 2000 cal BC, which provides a good general idea of the date of the salt extraction on the site, though the samples were apparently of charcoal and the calibration curve does not allow finer chronological resolution in this period.

Another site, Santioste, with Chalcolithic, Early and Middle Bronze Age pottery (but radiocarbon dates suggesting a Beaker date), produced much burnt clay, pits, and a number of "combustion structures" (Abarquero Moras *et al.* 2012: 222 ff.), as well as briquetage. These latter are elongated pits with clay linings fired pink and red and much evidence of firing debris. Similar structures, of a somewhat later (Iron Age) date, were recovered at Fuente Salina (Abarquero Moras *et al.* 2012: 275 ff.), though there was some debate as to whether this site was really a salt production place rather than merely domestic. How these structures functioned is a matter of some speculation, but it would appear that fires were lit in the pit, and briquetage trays or bowls placed over them; this assumes that the pits (trenches) were narrow enough for the trays to stay in place, or that some kind of other stand was placed across the trench (Abarquero Moras *et al.* 2012: 312 ff., Fig. 159)

Italy

Coastal Italy has seen a number of investigations in recent years into Bronze Age salt production. On the Tyrrhenian side, work by Marinella Pasquinucci and colleagues south of Pisa at Isola di Coltano, and by Peter Attema and colleagues near Nettuno in southern Lazio, has produced evidence in the form of burnt material associated with large quantities of pottery, and at Isola di Coltano cylindrical or square-sectioned firedogs (probably serving as pedestals in the boiling process) (Di Fraia & Secoli 2002; Nijboer *et al.* 2005/2006; Pasquinucci & Menchelli 2002). Di Fraia (2011) suggests that the medium-sized vessels at the site might have been used for solar evaporation, a crust of sodium chloride forming on the top of the brine and easily removed by hand. Bronze Age sites on the coast between Livorno and Populonia, and at the Saline di Volterra, probably suggest more intensive exploitation than survives today. At the Caput Adriae, work by Emanuela Montagnari Kokelj has found similar material at Stramare near the mouth of the river Ospo, the suggestion being that this was where preliminary brine concentration took place, the final processing happening at the castelliere of Elleri, where much briquetage is present (Cassola Guida & Montagnari Kokelj 2006; Montagnari Kokelj 2007). Occupation of Elleri extends, however, over a long period, from Middle Bronze Age to Late Iron Age. Historically many salt pans are known from the Caput Adriae, so there is nothing surprising here – except perhaps that semi-processed brine was taken so far away from the coast for turning into usable salt. As Cassola Guida and Montagnari Kokelj point out, the salt production activities found at present around the Gulf of Trieste are no doubt very ancient, even if it remains hard to be sure that the surviving evidence indicates Bronze Age production.

Mines and quarries

Mining and quarrying are related activities, depending on how deep into the ground the shafts or hollows go. Where salt outcrops on the surface, and no or minimal digging downwards is necessary, the procedure can generally be categorized as quarrying; mining, by contrast, typically involves the digging of shafts into the ground. The distinction is to some extent artificial, since "open-cast mining" (*Tagebau*) involves the removal of the overburden to expose the buried rock or ore, which can essentially then be quarried.

As far as the exploitation of rock salt in the Bronze Age was concerned, both mining and quarrying took place, but the only site with undisputed evidence for deep mining is Hallstatt in the Salzkammergut area of Austria. Elsewhere, notably in Romania where many exposures of rock salt occur on or near the earth's surface, quarrying is likely to have occurred even where no trace survives. Where rock salt occurs close to the surface, as in the Beclean area, excavation has shown that digging to remove the uppermost layers of salt by quarrying or mining took place, though this was supplemented by additional technological processes.

Hallstatt

Although Hallstatt is best known as an Iron Age site, it has long been known that there was an extensive Bronze Age presence there; one group of mine shafts dates almost exclusively to the Bronze Age. Earlier work produced radiocarbon dates from the "Northern group" of shafts that fall in the Late Bronze Age (Barth *et al.* 1975), while the campaigns of excavation that have taken place over the last twenty years have shown that three working areas, as well as other more isolated instances, have Bronze Age material: the Appoldwerk, Grünerwerk and most particularly the Christian von Tuschwerk (Kern *et al.* 2009: 50 ff.). Extraction in these areas has been dendrochronologically dated to 1458-1243 BC (Grabner *et al.* 2007; Grabner *et al.* 2006). Extraordinary detail is preserved in some of the shafts. The Appoldwerk seems to have had an elaborate scaffold arrangement to enable the miners to go deeper into the ground; the Grünerwerk was 23 x 7 m in cross-section, but apparently without planking to retain the walls of the shaft. Most remarkable of all was the finding in 2003 of a wooden ladder, or rather a staircase, in the Christian von Tuschwerk (Kern *et al.* 2009: 61-3), dated dendrochronologically to 1344-43 BC. This stairway is 1.20 m wide and 8 m long, and seems to have been designed to enable passage across heaps of mining spoil; parts of other, narrower, stairs were found elsewhere.

The extraction technique was by bronze picks to create deep parallel grooves in the rock salt surface (Fig. 6.4, 4), and then to hammer the intervening rock out in lumps or chips; these were then carried off in skin rucksacks and wooden trugs, remarkable examples of which survive (Fig. 6.4, 1). The material was then hoisted to the surface using ropes of lime bast, perhaps in woollen sacks.

At present the Hallstatt mines are the only ones certainly known to have used deep mining in the Bronze Age. At the Dürrnberg mines, some 40 km to the north-west of Hallstatt, all the evidence so far indicates an Iron Age date with nothing from the Bronze Age (Chapter 6). It is possible that deep mining for salt took place in the Transcarpathian area of Ukraine, but this is just as likely to been a form of opencasting, similar to what is known in Romania (see below).

The area over which the Hallstatt mines might have held economic sway in the Bronze Age was large; they might have supplied the western part of the Carpathian Basin (with Wieliczka potentially supplying the northern part, Transylvania the eastern, and Tuzla the southern – though this latter is pure speculation). South of the Alps, the salt lagoons of Volterra or the Caput Adriae would represent the nearest alternative suppliers, and as mentioned above, there is evidence for a Bronze Age interest at these sites. It must be admitted, however, that the economic position of Hallstatt in the Bronze Age has been less intensively studied than that in the Iron Age, even though it was assuredly a salt source of prime importance in both periods. This situation is now changing with the work of Hans Reschreiter and Kerstin Kowarik (see below, Chapter 9).

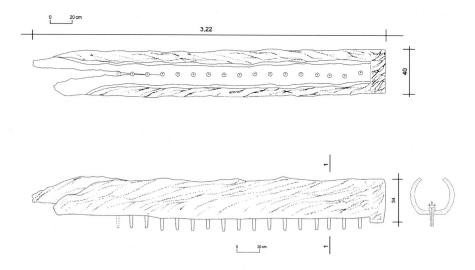

Fig. 5.5. Băile Figa, Beclean, Romania: trough (drawing: National Museum of the Eastern Carpathians, Sfîntu Gheorghe, Romania)

The trough technique

What I am here calling the "trough technique" has only become widely known in the last few years, though objects used in this type of salt production were first found in the early 19th century. The history of discovery has been described several times, most recently by Harding and Kavruk in the context of publishing their work in the Carpathian zone mainly in the years 2005-2010 (Harding 2011; Harding & Kavruk 2010; 2013). Wooden troughs (hollowed out tree-trunks, similar to log canoes or tree-trunk coffins) have been found in present-day Ukraine and in several places in Transylvania; at present nowhere else, though this geographical restriction seems quite unlikely, and similar finds from other areas may well emerge.

The troughs are highly unusual in that their bases are perforated with a row of holes (Fig. 5.5), and in those examples where preservation allows, the holes are filled with wooden plugs or pegs, themselves perforated; these perforations were filled with twisted cord or wooden needle-like splinters. None of the surviving troughs is complete, so it is unknown how many holes were originally present in the base, or whether both trough ends were enclosed or one end was left open.

The most complete evidence comes from the recent excavations at Băile Figa near Beclean in Romania, though even here the surviving evidence is incomplete and in many ways baffling. The troughs found on this site (to date six in number, in varying states of completeness, with possible fragments of others) lay in the mud of a brine stream, overlying rock salt, and seem to have been thrown aside during later episodes of production using different methods (Iron Age and early medieval). It is thus impossible to know exactly how they were mounted and used, but there is evidence to suggest that they were fastened by withy ties onto a wooden framework. Clearly liquids must have been introduced into the trough and allowed to drip

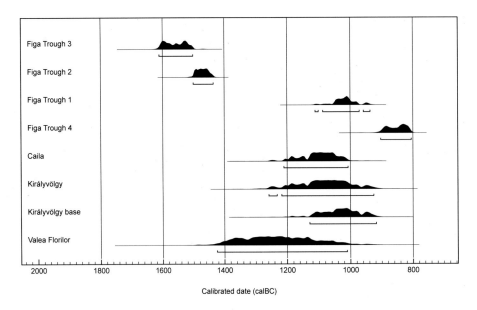

Figa Trough 3
Figa Trough 2
Figa Trough 1
Figa Trough 4
Caila
Királyvölgy
Királyvölgy base
Valea Florilor

2000   1800   1600   1400   1200   1000   800

Calibrated date (calBC)

Fig. 5.6. Radiocarbon dates for troughs in the Carpathian Basin (source: Harding & Kavruk 2013)

slowly through the holes at the bottom onto the rock salt below. Radiocarbon dates indicate that the troughs were made between the sixteenth and ninth centuries cal BC, and presumably used during all or part of that period.

Troughs are now known from at least four or possibly six other sites, in Romania and Ukraine. All are very similar, though there is variation in the shape of the pegs plugging the holes in the base of the trough: some are square or rectangular in cross-section, others are round. Radiocarbon dates suggest that the round version came first, and was replaced with the square version; it has been suggested that this was a technological development to stop the peg sliding round or through the hole, but to sit firmly in position.

Radiocarbon dates have been obtained on troughs from four sites (Fig. 5.6): Băile Figa and Caila (both Bistrița-Năsăud county), Valea Florilor (Cluj county), and the Ukrainian site formerly known as Királyvölgy (now near the modern village of Tisolovo, Tyachiv district). The earlier two of the four troughs at Figa date to the 16th-15th centuries cal BC, those from Caila and Királyvölgy to the 12th-11th, and the later troughs at Figa to the 11th to 9th centuries cal BC. The Valea Florilor date has too broad a range for any clear indication of chronological position to be established, other than that it belongs to the Bronze Age.

How this technique assisted the production of salt has been discussed a number of times. Two main theories hold sway. The first, suggested already in the 19th century after the discoveries in present-day Ukraine, is that fresh water was channeled into the trough and allowed to drip onto the hard rock salt surface, forming depressions and grooves which could then be enlarged by wedges hammered into the rock, allowing chunks of rock to be detached. The second theory supposes that brine was introduced into the trough for concentration, the drips collected in a container

Fig. 5.7. Wooden installations at Băile Figa, Beclean, Romania, probably for storing and filtering brine (photo: V. Kavruk)

beneath or allowed to form crystals that could be collected, for instance from a textile placed underneath. Experiments have shown that the first method works quite well (Buzea 2010), at least as far as breaking up the rock salt is concerned; the second also works, though no full-scale reconstruction has yet been conducted (Harding 2009).

Troughs were, however, only part of the story. Contemporary with them were a range of other constructions, notably wattle fences but also structures made of planks and poles, in some cases apparently roofed (Fig. 5.7). It is believed that all these constructions were intended to store brine, perhaps with the addition of the chunks of rock salt produced by the troughs in order to increase the salt concentration of the water and make crystallization easier and quicker. A similar technique was used at Hallstatt from the medieval period on, and can be seen on visits to the site today; brine evaporation rather than simply rock extraction became the norm there once production picked up in the Renaissance, and continued until salt-boiling in the pan-houses stopped in 1964.

The latest evidence from Băile Figa (excavations by Valeriu Cavruc in August 2013) has brought together many of the features previously found in isolation in different excavation trenches. A trench in the middle of the site (Trench XV) has produced three troughs, with a fourth found close by some years earlier; immediately beside these troughs were a ladder and a round wattle enclosure, replaced at least once. Large channelled pieces were beside the troughs, most likely to bring water into them. While so far only two of the troughs have been dated (to the Bronze Age), wattle fences elsewhere on the site were also of that date, and the ladder, though undated, is of different construction to the Iron Age example found in the southern area of the site. What seems most likely is that the troughs were used in a production line or chain, and the wattle enclosures were for brine storage, presumably lined with clay to make them more or less watertight.

While the precise method by which the troughs and associated structures were used still remains somewhat unclear, what is certain is that the scale of the operation was significant, especially at Băile Figa, where most information is available, but potentially also at other contemporary sites in and beyond Transylvania. With constructions stretching at Figa over an area some 500 m long north to south, and 200 m east to west in places, the operation was big, even allowing for a trend over time from south to north (as radiocarbon dates show). It has been argued that this type of production, at least at this location, was industrial in scale – that is, it was intended for far more than merely domestic use in local communities. Certainly by comparison with briquetage use in the Bronze Age, the output must have been very much greater. I return to these matters below.

The Bronze Age – summary

Bronze Age salt has until recently been something of a Cinderella subject, taking second or even third place to Iron Age and Neolithic production. The foregoing discussion should have made it clear that this situation has now changed radically, with extensive information available from certain parts of Europe for a range of production methods, some of them capable of producing very large amounts of salt. Of course there must have also been other production sites using techniques which leave no archaeological trace, such as salt lagoons; it is reasonable to assume that these existed in many parts of Europe, especially round the Mediterranean. The extent to which salt became a major feature of the Bronze Age economy I shall consider in a later chapter.

Chapter 6

The Iron Age: Austrian mines, French briquetage, English Red Hills and other sites

With the Iron Age, broadly speaking the first millennium BC, we enter a new chapter in European salt production. Instead of hypotheses about likely sources and techniques, or reconstructions of ill-understood installations, the archaeological material at our disposal is abundant and for the most part well understood. It is also the time when the civilisations of Greece and Rome rose to prominence, with all that that entails in terms of economic flourishing and technological mastery. Although, as discussed above in Chapter 3, there is much that is not known about salt production in Greece and Rome, this is probably because it was considered so obvious to the writers on whose testimony we depend that they did not think it worth recording. In fact everything we know or can reconstruct about Iron Age salt production indicates that it achieved massive proportions in many areas of Europe.

There follows a brief summary of the evidence from each area of Europe; this makes no pretence at completeness, because the literature is extensive and the numbers of sites huge. It is in the Iron Age that most salt-related fieldwork is taking place at the present day, so that the situation is changing rapidly, year by year.[23]

In the Iron Age, the technology of salt production became less varied than in the Bronze Age, in the sense that three main techniques were in use: solar evaporation in coastal lagoons, mining and quarrying, and brine boiling using briquetage. But this simple statement disguises the fact that there was an enormous increase in the use of briquetage for salt boiling, especially in Germany, France, and Britain, and very considerable variation in the form of the briquetage over time and space. In fact, in those countries, and probably in others as well, the briquetage technique was virtually the only one in use. To say that, however, is to ignore the abundant site evidence for installations, sometimes large in scale, that enabled industrial or quasi-industrial quantities of salt to be produced. The enormous increase in production evidenced by sites over much of central and western Europe where

---

23   It must be admitted, however, that some of the relevant literature is not easy to find, since it appeared in exhibition catalogues, local journals, or the proceedings of small conferences. A further problem is that of "grey literature" – reports produced by archaeological field units for commercial clients and never published in the academic press.

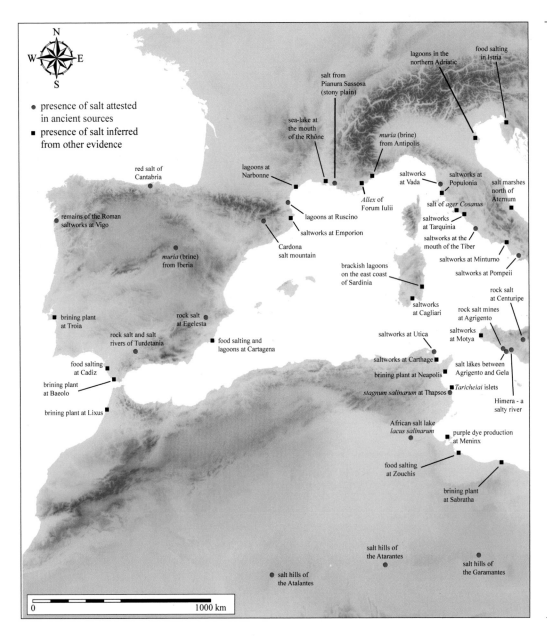

Fig. 6.1. Salt sources in the Graeco-Roman world (redrawn after Carusi 2008)

there are salt deposits has also enabled scholars to speculate on implications for economy and society, matters to which I shall return in Chapters 8 and 9.

Lagoons and salt-pans: Greece and Rome

Cristina Carusi (2008: 49-148) has listed the locations where salt production can be assumed or demonstrated, using both textual, toponymic, and archaeological sources. The quality of the evidence naturally varies, but in general it is possible

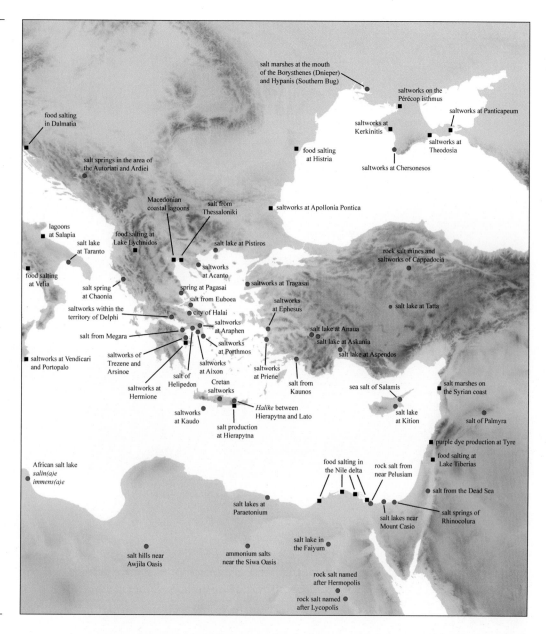

to reconstruct an extensive network of salterns, mainly pans and lagoons, around Mediterranean shores and in some cases inland (Fig. 6.1). Many of these coastal sources are still in production today, some probably on the very same spots where Roman production took place (Fig. 6.2). While in most cases one cannot show that these sources were active in earlier centuries, it would be surprising if they were not known to the prehistoric occupants of the area, and thus utilised for both human and animal needs.

Fig. 6.2. Salt pans on Pelješac, Croatia (photo: Jasmina, Dreamstime.com)

Fig. 6.3. Aerial view of Hallstatt showing the lake and Mount Plassen. The small valley in front of the mountain is the salt valley (photo: Luftbildarchiv Institut für Ur- und Frühgeschichte Wien)

Mining and quarrying

The salt mines of Hallstatt (Fig. 6.3) have already figured prominently in the previous chapter. But in the Iron Age they achieved their greatest extent and widest fame, not just because of the technology involved in the mining operation but also because of the famous cemetery with its rich graves, covering the earlier stages of the Iron Age (Ha C and D). A few graves date to the preceding Urnfield period, Ha A and B, but their numbers are relatively insignificant; but they probably reflect the fact that mining resumed at the site around 900 BC.

At Hallstatt new shafts were opened in the Iron Age, expanding the exploited area several-fold – but only after a gap in activity lasting 300 years or more, on the radiocarbon and dendro evidence (Grabner *et al.* 2006). The Iron Age technology was different from that used in the Bronze Age, where more or less vertical shafts were sunk; now horizontal adits were cut into the hillside to follow the veins of salt (Kern *et al.* 2009: 84 ff.; Stöllner 1999: 36 ff.). The galleries thus formed were very large. Bronze picks continued to be used, however, and heart-shaped blocks of salt were prised off the rock surfaces, apparently weighing up to 100 kg each, with smaller chips and spalls of salt simply being left on the gallery floor. Spruce and fir tapers were used to light the work underground; huge numbers of these were also found in excavations at the Dürrnberg. Large amounts of organic material survive from the Iron Age levels explored, which have given unrivalled insights into daily life of the miners (Fig. 6.4).

Activity in the Early Iron Age part of the mine came to an end, perhaps sudden, in the middle of the 4th century BC, when rock falls and inflow of fine sediment filled the galleries and shafts (Kern *et al.* 2009: 156 ff.). Activity moved further up the hill, where adits were cut in the Dammwiese in the La Tène period (2nd century BC). This area has been extensively damaged by historic and modern mining, so little is known about it, but it appears to have been extensive. By this time, however, activity at the Dürrnberg was advanced. The two mining areas together must have produced enormous quantities of rock salt, which was no doubt moved far and wide, north and south of the Alps.

Extensive modern excavations at the Dürrnberg have taken place, with dendrochronology and finds evidence showing exploitation from the fifth century BC onwards; the various mining areas were worked through to the late La Tène period (Stöllner 1999; 2002; 2003). The deep shafts here have again produced huge quantities of organic material. Also here are signs of "catastrophes", in the form of an influx of sediments in flooding events; a massive event of this kind took place in the second half of the 4th century BC (dendro-dated) (Stöllner 2003: 136-7 Fig. 10). Here too it has been possible to suggest how salt fitted in to the local economy (below, chapter 8).

The mining, or rather quarrying, of rock salt was not confined to these Alpine areas, however. Recent work in Romania has shown that rock salt extraction was undertaken at least at Băile Figa by means of digging shafts down to the surface of the rock, through the debris of earlier production by the trough technique (Harding & Kavruk 2013). The rock lies several metres below the modern ground surface, but was presumably less deep in prehistory before quarrying took place.

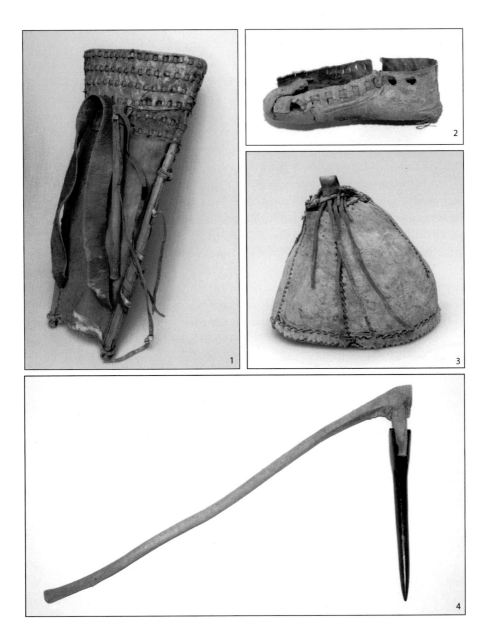

Fig. 6.4. Objects from the Hallstatt salt mines. 1. Bronze Age backpack of cow hide; 2. Early Iron Age shoe; 3. Bronze Age cap; 4. Bronze Age bronze pick (photos: A. Rausch, Naturhistorisches Museum, Wien)

Nevertheless, of the shafts found one was lined with split timbers, braced with cross-members, and the other, unlined, contained a ladder over 5 m in length, obviously for stepping down into the shaft (Fig. 6.5). Both the ladder and the lining of the shaft were radiocarbon dated to the fourth and third centuries BC (calibrated).

It is possible that other Transylvanian sites also saw comparable activity in the Iron Age. A site at Sânpaul in Harghita county, with visible timbers in a salty stream, produced a single radiocarbon date in the Early Iron Age; the place is supposed to have been the site of Roman salt production (an inscription on a votive altar nearby refers to a *conductor salinarum*, the manager of a saltworks), but apart from the presence of a Roman fort and *vicus* nearby there is no other evidence for Roman salt mining. Taken together with the abundant evidence for prehistoric interest in Moldavian and Transylvanian salt, and the several Roman inscriptions from the province comparable to that just mentioned, it is highly likely that Roman exploitation occurred in many spots, and that these were where Dacian Iron Age exploitation had also occurred.

Salt-boiling using briquetage

As mentioned above, it was during the Iron Age that the briquetage technique of producing salt really came into its own. Across a wide swathe of northern Europe, from England to Germany, numerous production sites were created in this period, based on the evaporation of brine using furnaces with more or less elaborate superstructures above, on which pans or trays of brine were placed. Some of these were quite simple, as appears to have been the case on many of the English sites; others were highly complex, as in France; some made use of seawater, others brine from springs. The principle appears to have been the same in all areas, however; to boil off the water and end up with crystalline salt.

France

France saw a huge amount of salt production in the Iron Age, with several sites providing very well-preserved evidence for the technology involved. French scholars have written extensively about the topic in recent years, on the basis of highly informative and well-conducted excavations. As a result, much is known about the technological processes involved in salt production in the French Iron Age. Many areas and sites have been studied, but two stand out particularly: Lorraine, and in particular the Seille valley (Marsal, Moyenvic); and the line of the A16 motorway through the Pas-de-Calais and Somme départements. For the former the work of Laurent Olivier, building on earlier studies by Bertaux and others, has revealed an industrial landscape in extraordinary detail (Bertaux 1976; 1977; Olivier 2000 (2001); 2005; 2007; 2010; Olivier & Kovacik 2006; Poncelet 1966); while for the latter the work of Olivier Weller and Gilles Prilaux, using excavation data from Yves Desfossés and others, have given the world a highly detailed description and analysis of salt production near the Channel coast (O. Weller in Desfossés 2000: 272-280, 333-353; Prilaux 2000; Prilaux *et al.* 2011). It would be otiose to repeat the observations of these scholars in more than brief outline, since they have essentially lifted the lid on the workings of a complex but widespread technology found in many parts of France in the Iron Age. Detailed work has been done on

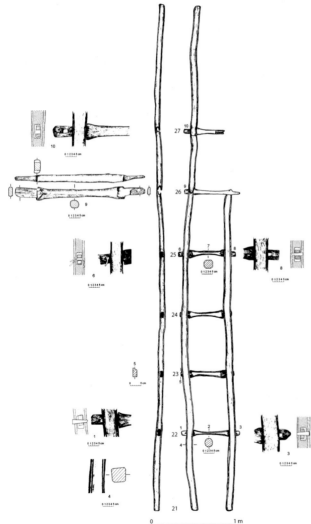

Fig. 6.5. Wooden ladder from Băile Figa, Beclean, Romania. Above: in situ during excavation (photo: Author); below: drawing after removal (drawing: Tamás Baranus)

Brittany by Marie-Yvane Daire and colleagues (Daire 1994); this author has also produced a very useful summarising survey (2003), bringing in results from other areas on the Atlantic coast in addition to the Channel sites mentioned.

The Seille valley

Work in the Seille valley in Lorraine goes back to the 18th century; indeed, it was the engineer Félix-François Le Royer Artézé de la Sauvagère who coined the term "briquetage" in 1740 on seeing the mounds of brick-like material in the Marsal and Moyenvic areas – what we now know are the fired clay remnants of evaporation furnaces. Modern work started in the 1970s, but it was only with the creation of the latest programme of work in 2001 that the most spectacular results have emerged. As well as extensive survey by remote sensing and ground-based magnetometry, excavation at Marsal has produced enormous ranges of furnaces and other installations (Figs 6.6a, 6.6b). Olivier has shown that there are two main phases of activity in the Seille valley: 8th to 6th centuries BC (Ha C-D1), and 2nd-1st centuries BC (LT D); the industrial quantities of waste briquetage belong mainly to the late period (Olivier 2000 (2001); 2005; 2010; Olivier & Kovacik 2006). A typological development of the briquetage containers fits into this chronology (Olivier 2005: 222 ff., Fig. 5).

Initially the brine emerging from springs and wells was heated and evaporated in large pottery basins or troughs to form a concentrated saline paste; this material was then formed into cakes or ingots using a second furnace with a griddle of fired clay bars. Onto this griddle were placed the moulds which contained the concentrated brine. The moulds themselves took on a fixed range of forms, and in the late Iron Age phase of exploitation took on a uniform shape. Olivier estimates that in the earlier production phase hundreds to thousands of tonnes of salt may have been produced, but in the late phase thousands to tens of thousands of tonnes. The scale of production was thus enormous, and can be considered industrial in scale.

Atlantic and Channel coasts

There is a long history of study of salt-making sites along the western coasts of France. The work of Michel Tessier and Pierre Louis Gouletquer laid the foundations in the 1960s and 70s (Gouletquer 1969; 1970; Tessier 1960), while Jean-Claude Hocquet has since produced a number of important studies (Hocquet 1986; 1994; 2001). These have shown, among other things, that the briquetage developed over the course of the Iron Age and into the Gallo-Roman period, and that the type of exploitation also changed: from "domestic" (household production), through "artisan" (workshop production) to "industrial". These matters were also considered by Marie-Yvane Daire and colleagues (Daire 1994: 100 ff.), and I return to them in Chapter 9 (p. 121).

Recent studies have confirmed that very large numbers of salt production sites dating to the Late Iron Age or Gallo-Roman period are present along France's western coasts; Weller gives the figure as over 300, admitting that many more sites

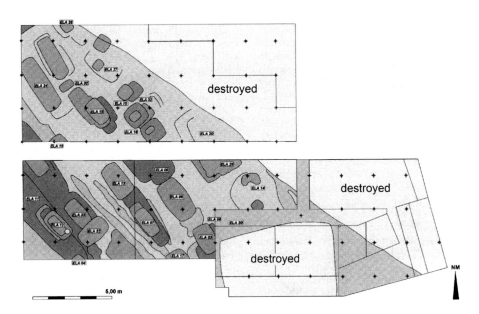

Fig. 6.6a. Marsal "la Digue" (Seille valley, Lorraine): plan of brine storage tanks ("structures artisanales") (source: Olivier 2010)

Fig. 6.6b. Excavation in progress on the salt production site at Marsal, showing the U-shaped furnaces for brine evaporation which appear in long rows (photo: Laurent Olivier)

must have been lost (in Desfossés 2000: 336). Many of these seem to have exploited salty sand or mud rather than seawater, but the end product was probably much the same since the sand would have to be saturated with water and then boiled. What is involved is the process known as lixiviation (the separation of soluble from insoluble substances by dissolving the soluble part in water). This has implications for the type of furnace employed, however, since the sand or mud would have to be removed after boiling and deposited elsewhere. The *chaîne opératoire* involved is considered in Chapter 9.

Work along the line of the A16 motorway in the Pas-de-Calais and Somme has found a series of sites, notably at Sorrus just outside Étaples (Desfossés 2000: 215 ff.), where sunken oval hearths or furnaces were reconstructed as having the characteristic griddle form, onto which pans and trays were put (Fig. 6.7). Beside the hearth, wattle-lined wells and pits for storing brine were found; the wells had silted up and briquetage was found in the upper layers; the date range of the site is quite broad, the pottery spanning several La Tène phases, but dendro dates indicate a focus on the third century BC. Weller's study of the briquetage (in Desfossés 2000: 272 ff.) showed that a standard range of forms was present, consisting of beakers (moulds), supports (pedestals and so-called "hand-bricks"; these are mini-pedestals, squeezed by hand and placed between two troughs or pans, similar to what in Britain are now called spacers or clips) (Daire 1994: 76 Fig. 53), and structural elements from the furnace lining and griddle. There was some difference in the distribution of the containers and the furnace elements, presumably indicating that the moulds were removed from the furnace after it had cooled down and then broken up to remove the salt. Weller was also able to suggest a two-stage development of the briquetage process: the first running to the end of the 4th century or beginning of the 3rd, in which more or less circular structures were in use, with supports surmounted by beakers in red sandy fabric; and a second from the 3rd century with rectangular ovens and a griddle; this became a standard form in the following decades, down to around 150 BC. Geographical differences are also detectable over this large area; Weller identifies no less than six (ibid. 350-1).

Further south, near Abbeville, Gilles Prilaux has studied sites with comparable installations, for instance at Pont-Rémy, and derived a similar detailed typology both of the briquetage and of the furnaces (Prilaux 2000). Comparable typologies have been developed by a number of other French authors (reviewed by Daire 2003: 32 ff.).

Recent work has identified a further range of sites along the coasts of Lower Normandy, from the Mont-Saint-Michel bay, around the Cotentin peninsula, and along the north coast of Lower Normandy to the Seine (Carpentier et al. 2012). Here too it has been possible to derive a typological development of production installations through the Iron Age, from furnaces with slabs surmounted by pedestals supporting cylindrical containers at the time of the Hallstatt-La Tène transition around 450 BC, to a range of types involving troughs, hand-bricks (clips), and eventually griddle constructions during the successive centuries of La Tène.

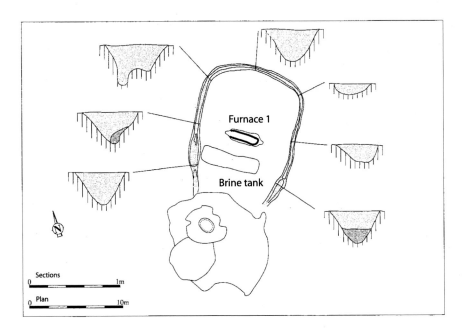

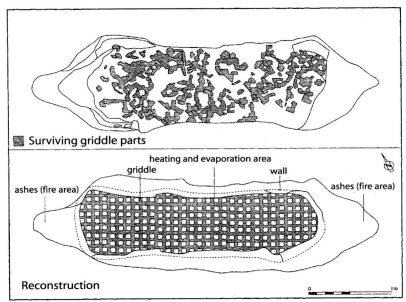

Fig. 6.7. Plan and reconstruction of Furnace 1 from Sourus "La Bruyère". Upper: general plan; lower: surviving furnace parts and reconstruction (source: Desfossés 2000)

In Brittany a range of sites producing briquetage are present, studied earlier by Pierre Louis Gouletquer (1970), more recently by Marie-Yvane Daire (1994; 2003: 72 ff.). Gouletquer identified a range of briquetage forms (such as trumpet-shaped, T-shaped and tripod pedestals), but inevitably at that time dating was insecure. Gouletquer was able to show how widespread the griddle-type of furnace supporting moulds was ("fours à augets"), and produced the first detailed study of the Trégor area, with its connections to the Chausey and Channel islands, and Finistère. In essence, all these sites consist of a furnace, with wells for obtaining water and storage pits for brine, though the specific layout may vary from site to site and area to area. In Aquitaine too a series of sites have been found (summarised by Daire 2003: 91 ff.) but also considered by Gouletquer. Here, areas such as the Marais Poitevin or the Saintonge area are particularly prolific in briquetage sites.

The large number of sites on or near the French coast, and the variability between them, makes any detailed description redundant, since most have already been excellently presented in the recent literature.

Germany

In Germany a number of areas have provided extensive evidence for salt production in the Iron Age, perhaps none more so than Bad Nauheim in Hesse (first modern study: Jorns 1960). The town lies on the foothills of the Taunus mountains in the Wetterau district, on the Usa (a small river flowing into the Wetter, and thence to the Nidda, which joins the Main in Frankfurt). Extensive salt workings in historical times have forerunners in the Roman period and the Iron Age, the brine springs containing 2-4% salt. Archaeological investigations have taken place over many years; the first traces of Iron Age salt working were discovered in 1837 (Kull 2003a), and rescue work has continued up to the present day. Numerous evaporation furnaces have turned up, whole or partial, with extensive areas of burning; much was early medieval in date, including stone troughs, wooden tanks and lead collection pans. Of the Roman presence in Bad Nauheim, circular collection areas made of wattle (*Faschinengruben*) in the area known as "Auf dem Siebel", in the area of the southern saltworks, are of particular interest, recalling as they do the Bronze Age installations at Băile Figa (see above) (Kull 2003a, 140-1, Abb. 65-67). The La Tène presence is still more important in the present context. Extensive settlement and craft workshop remains were found at several parts of the town, but it is the salt-working remains that are of particular importance. Again, it is in the southern part of town that the most important remains turned up: including wattle fences, wooden box-like shafts, channels, troughs and portable objects (that have been dendro-dated to the second and early first centuries BC) (Kull 2003a, 156 ff.). Isolated finds of briquetage (pedestals, beakers etc) show that this method was also used.[24]

In Kurstrasse, a large area was opened and a remarkable series of installations discovered (Bettwieser 2003; Kull 2003a). Together with the findings from 'Auf dem Siebel', they constitute one of the best sets of Iron Age salt workings from anywhere in Europe. The whole ensemble in Kurstrasse is dated to the third and second centuries BC. As well as wattle fences, wood channels and troughs, there was a remarkable series of stone paved areas, roughly square, with wooden collection boxes; many of the wooden pieces had sintering traces on them in the form of a lime deposit from the brine. On or under the stone paving were large clay-covered

---

24 For the elongated rectangular shape of the ovens there are Hallstatt forerunners at Löbnitz-Bennewitz, 3 x 1.5 m in size with pedestal and brick-shaped briquetage (Preier 1997 [1999]).

basins, containing oven debris and small pieces of briquetage. The suggestion is that the pavements served as conserving areas, making use of the brine, though this would not explain the overflow function of the wooden boxes. The stone pavements have a depression in the middle, and the connecting pipes on the wood boxes lie at an angle so that the overflow from the pavement would be siphoned off. An alternative suggestion is that in winter some kind of concentration process was being attempted – the presence of broken stones might suggest the application of heat.

Other sites where Iron Age salt exploitation can be securely demonstrated include Bad Mergentheim in the Tauber valley of northern Baden-Württemberg (Simon 1995: 66 ff.), and Schwäbisch Hall (Hees 1999; 2012; Simon 1995: 79 ff.) east of Heilbronn. This last is particularly interesting because of the range of installations found on the site, including wattle-lined brine storage pits and wooden troughs, the largest being 5 m long, 1.2 m wide and 50 cm deep.[25] Opinions have varied over how these troughs functioned; earlier ideas were that they were intended as some kind of grading device for concentrating brine, perhaps by means of inserting heated ceramic pieces (which were indeed found inside some of them). As well as these wooden objects, large quantities of briquetage were found, mainly containers, slabs, and conical or triangular-section supports.

At Werl, Kreis Soest, in Westphalia, there is extensive evidence that shows the existence of Iron Age exploitation of the salt sources (Leidinger 1983; 1996). Recent work has shown that this dates exclusively to the Early Iron Age (Laumann 2000). This is to say nothing of the situation in north Germany, in the Hannover area or near Lüneburg, where the rich salt sources were surely exploited in prehistory as they were in historic periods.

Low Countries

Sites on the North Sea coast in Belgium and the Netherlands have been known for many years. Among the most famous are De Panne and Bray-Dunes on the French-Belgian border (De Ceunynck & Thoen 1981; Kerger 1999; Leman-Delerive *et al.* 1996; Nenquin 1961: 93-5; Thoen 1975), where large quantities of briquetage are present, dating to the end of the Iron Age but not, according to Thoen, the Roman period, when a different technology was in use. Salt-making at De Panne was probably conducted on a level sandy area protected from the sea by dunes, but given the shifting nature of the shore in such an area this is somewhat uncertain.

In recent years many more sites have produced evidence for salt production; these have been assembled and studied by Peter van den Broeke (1995; 1996; 2007). He has shown that specific forms of briquetage occur not only at coastal sites but also inland: the so-called "solid briquetage" (pedestals and the like), which is found close to the sea, and half-cylinders (cylindrical vessels cut or split along the long axis), which occur at many locations near Oss (site of the famous grave

---

25 Although these troughs are superficially similar to those found at Băile Figa (see above), they differ significantly in not having perforations in the base; their function was therefore different.

dating to Ha C) and in adjacent parts of the Rhineland (Simons 1987), indicating trade in salt from the coast to the interior.

England

Iron Age salt-making on the east coast of England has been much studied, and over many decades. As discussed in Chapter 1, the study of the "Red Hills" found on the coasts of eastern England goes back to the 19th century, and continued through the 20th, with a series of studies shedding light on the matter.[26] Recent excavation and survey has shed much light on the distribution of sites and the methods of production, thanks above all to the work of Tom Lane and Elaine Morris (2001) in the Fenland areas of Lincolnshire and Cambridgeshire; their publication of 2001 represents a milestone in archaeological salt studies in England, considering, as they do, not only how and when salt was produced, but also the implications of that production for the economy and society of the areas and periods involved.

The study of Red Hills started in Essex (the coastal areas east and north-east of London) (Fig. 3.3). A long history of exploration and study (reviewed in Kinory 2012: 4 ff.) culminated in a systematic, though brief, study published in 1990 (Fawn *et al.* 1990, with full references to earlier work), updated somewhat in 1995 (Sealey 1995). Over 300 sites are known in Essex alone, and some the other side of the Thames estuary in Kent, though many of these are Roman in date. Modern excavations have been few, so that the knowledge of the internal structure of the mounds is not as good as it might be; but it is clear that they contain hearths (furnaces), pits or tanks for brine storage and settling, flues, and abundant briquetage – containers, supports, "firebars" (part of a griddle arrangement on which the containers were placed), and other small pieces (wedges, "pinch props" – spacer-clips in the terminology of Elaine Morris – and rods). How these were all arranged into an effective brine-boiling system is less clear; in essence they involved creating a structure with fire beneath and supports for containers above, but it must be admitted that the evidence from Essex is much less clear than from corresponding sites on the Continent. The most recent work in the area (Biddulph *et al.* 2012, Chapter 4) confirms this picture.

Typical installations of the Iron Age may be seen at Helpringham Fen in Lincolnshire (H. Healey in Bell *et al.* 1999). This site produced abundant briquetage in the form of bricks and plates, pyramidal pieces, props, bridges, bars and vessel fragments, associated with rectangular hearths surrounded by ditches, with much ash and other firing debris (Fig. 6.8). The briquetage is similar to that from a Roman site at Holbeach St Johns (D. Gurney in Bell *et al.* 1999).[27]

At other sites, the standard production method was to create some form of hearth or furnace, typically in an elongated pit, with supports holding up evaporation pans for the boiling of brine. In this there are obvious similarities to what is found in France, though the scale is much smaller. At one site, Cowbit Wash, it appears that both troughs and pans of various shapes were used simultaneously

---

26 Interestingly, one of the most informative accounts comes from a German scholar: Riehm 1961.
27 The classification is that by David Gurney (loc. cit.).

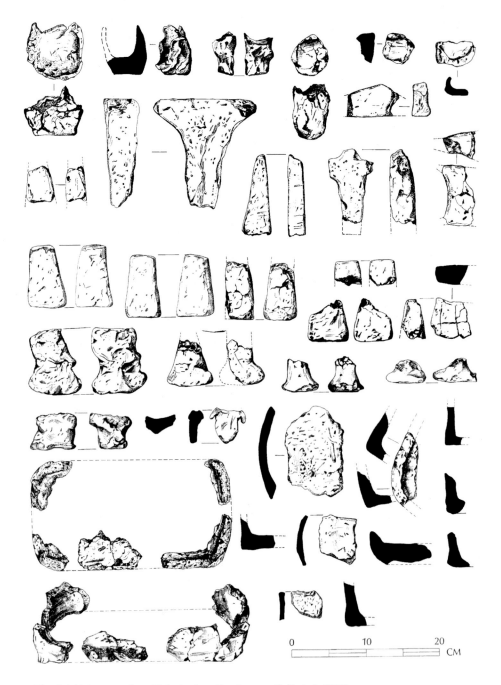

Fig. 6.8. Briquetage from Helpringham Fen (source: Bell et al. 1999)

in a multiple firing operation; at this one site alone, 24.5 kg of briquetage was recovered (Lane & Morris 2001: 33 ff.). The site dates to the late pre-Roman Iron Age. Other sites produced comparable quantities of material and enabled the authors to create a systematic typology of the briquetage from the Fenland sites, showing how it changed over time in terms of both form and of fabric, shelly limestone gritted temper being prevalent in the earlier material and organic in the later (Roman) phases, and individual types of container and support assignable to specific centuries (Lane & Morris 2001: 351 ff.).

The situation in Somerset in south-west England is similar to that in Essex, with salt-working sites only becoming frequent in the Roman period (Leech 1977; 1981: 30 ff.), though there was Bronze Age activity at Brean Down (chapter 5).

Briquetage has been found quite frequently also in north-east England, notably on settlement sites. Steven Willis has demonstrated that briquetage is present in small quantities on around one quarter of excavated sites in the Tees valley and beyond, for instance at the Tofts Field, Stanwick (Willis in Fitts et al. 1999; Willis forthcoming). Further north, recent excavation of an enclosure at Berwick upon Tweed recovered 89 fragments of briquetage, most in a fine sandy fabric and represented by containers and one support or stabiliser (E.L. Morris in Proctor 2012: 52-78, Fig. 24); the site lay on an eroding cliff, part of which lies over 60 m above sea level, which raises the question of whether salt production was taking place beside the sea, on the cliff above it, or both. Excavation of a site at Street House on the Cleveland coast also produced saltworking material: ovens or furnaces full of burnt stones and briquetage, with pits close by for storing brine (Sherlock & Vyner 2013). Fragments of salt containers were visible in the top of the oven, and a range of vessels, supports (bars and pedestals) and a slab base in the bottom of the structure, with radiocarbon dates indicating exploitation at the very end of the pre-Roman Iron Age. Again, the workings took place high above the sea, here at an altitude of 170 m; why this should be is a matter of continuing interest. The prevalence of salt production on domestic sites of the Late Iron Age in north-east England has been associated with the rise of new farming practices at the time, but this remains speculative.

While these eastern areas have produced the largest number of sites, other areas of England should not be forgotten, notably Droitwich in the English Midlands and Middlewich and Northwich in Cheshire to the north-west. At Droitwich, excavation recovered plentiful briquetage associated with brine tanks lined with clay and oak boards or stakes, and hearths (Woodiwiss 1992). The brine at Droitwich is highly salt-saturated (25%); specific pottery types were created in order to transport the resulting salt to locations across western England and Wales; another specific pot type was used for salt from Cheshire sources, the location of which remains uncertain (Morris 1985; 1994). The distribution of these types has now been supplemented by the work of Janice Kinory (2012: 32 ff.), who has argued that most salt was distributed in archaeologically invisible containers, since so many Iron Age sites have no sign of briquetage, even where it might be expected on other grounds. At Middlewich a brine evaporation hearth, a timber-lined well

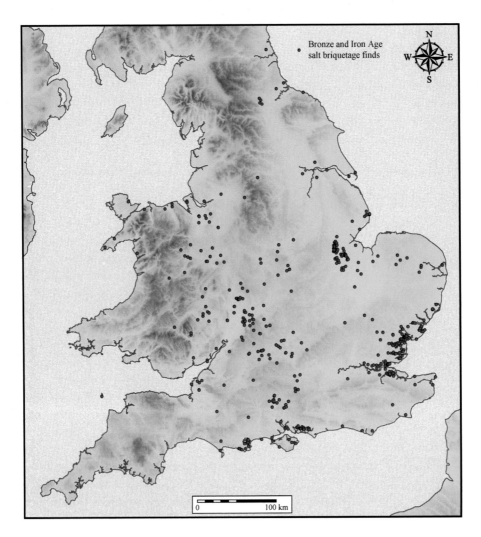

Fig. 6.9. Map of salt sites of Bronze and Iron Age date (source: Kinory 2012)

and a wattle-lined pit, dating to the first centuries BC and AD, were excavated along with a sizeable quantity of briquetage (Williams & Reid 2008).

Iron Age salt exploitation is also attested on and near the south coast of England, as is shown in Dorset by the presence of potential production sites (Farrar 1975) and by finds of briquetage at major emporia and hillforts such as Hengistbury Head and Danebury (fully referenced by Kinory 2012). There is some evidence from Sussex (Bradley 1975) but little has emerged in recent years (map of sites in Kinory 2012: 19-21 Fig. 10) (Fig. 6.9).

Taken all in all, there is extensive evidence from various parts of England, but in general the scale of exploitation at individual sites seems very much smaller than those across the Channel in France, especially eastern France.

The Iron Age: summary

It is evident from the foregoing that the Iron Age in Europe saw an enormous increase in salt production activity by comparison with that in the Bronze Age. Within the period, too, the amount of activity progressively increased, so that by the first century BC many parts of northern and western Europe were engaged in a high level of production, in some places on an industrial scale. Many of these places can be assumed or demonstrated to have engaged in the movement of salt in trade (this has often been suggested for Hallstatt, and is now apparent in coastal France and the Low Countries, and from the Droitwich and Cheshire sources in England). This raises many questions about the position of salt in the economy, and the extent to which it really served as "White Gold", the name which is often assigned to it. I return to these questions in Chapter 8.

Chapter 7

The development of salt working through European prehistory

The first certain evidence for salt production in Europe comes from the Neolithic. It has been suggested that one can infer a Mesolithic interest in salt-producing areas, but this is hypothetical: it is quite likely that people who settled in areas where salt springs or rock salt were present would make use of them.

The same is no doubt true for earlier periods as well, but the evidence there is completely absent. It would be all too easy to look at distribution maps of Palaeolithic sites or finds and "correlate" them with salt sources; but realistically any such correlation would almost certainly be matter of chance. A cluster of such sites in close proximity to a major salt source, with few or none further away, might be more telling, but to my knowledge no such situation is currently known.

As discussed in Chapter 4, the earliest certain salt production sites are those in the east of Romania, associated with Criş culture pottery. Interestingly, these sites appear to come with briquetage already fully formed, as at Cacica and Lunca. This raises the question: where did the technology come from? Where are the initial experimental stages of salt boiling? Even if the Mesolithic cases claimed by French scholars can be confirmed, they are ambiguous as far as the technology involved is concerned (though it appears that they involved the lighting of fires). In any case, there is nothing to link the south of France with the east of Romania. On present knowledge, the briquetage technique was invented somewhere east of the Carpathians early in the Neolithic.

In the ensuing centuries and millennia of the Neolithic, salt production appears in many different parts of Europe, from Transcaucasia in the east to Catalonia in the west, but with most evidence coming from Romania, Bulgaria and Poland. The evidence from Provadia is particularly impressive, particularly in the fifth millennium BC; the large brine pits and huge quantities of pottery seem to suggest production on a significant scale, even if questions remain about how such thin-walled pottery could have served for brine evaporation – perhaps they were used for the drying of salt crystals rather than boiling brine. The evidence from Cardona in the fifth and fourth millennia BC is also intriguing, though here it is proxy in nature rather than direct. Taken as a whole, however, one can be in no doubt that over the course of some four thousand years, or perhaps a little more, salt production became established in a range of different parts of Europe, setting the scene for developments over the latter millennia BC.

In the Copper and Bronze Ages, our knowledge of salt production starts with something of a lacuna. Taking the third millennium as a whole, one has to admit that there is little specific evidence anywhere, other than some isolated radiocarbon dates that suggest activity was proceeding (for instance at Băile Figa, Romania). Not until the appearance of numerous briquetage sites in the Halle area of Germany in the centuries around 2000 BC, and a range of production sites of Beaker and Early Bronze Age date in Spain, is there significant evidence anywhere. With that, however, salt production starts to appear in many parts of Europe, with briquetage sites across northern temperate Europe from Britain to Poland, solar evaporation of seawater taking place along Italian shores, and complicated wooden installations becoming the norm in the Carpathian Basin and probably beyond. While there are still significant gaps in knowledge in certain areas, and some technologies are imperfectly understood, it is the case that during the Bronze Age organised salt production becomes an everyday matter in many areas, and in some – I have suggested Transylvania as one of these – that production arguably reached industrial proportions. It was at this time also that Hallstatt started to produce salt in quantity, with extensive evidence for highly organised extraction arrangements involving a range of specialists to provide the necessary materials for the mining operation. The scene was set for what then happened in the second half of the first millennium BC.

In the Iron Age, salt exploitation took off in a big way. At the start of the period, the 8th century, it is mainly in Austria that we have extensive evidence, from the mines at Hallstatt. Within a few hundred years, and by the turn of Hallstatt to La Tène, things changed dramatically: between about 450 BC and the turn of the era, and especially by the first century BC, large numbers of places (and therefore people) were engaged in salt production. In the Mediterranean there is literary evidence to show this (even though traces on the ground are harder to spot); in western Europe, brine-boiling using briquetage became very common in many areas with rich salt sources. The Iron Age could almost be termed the Age of Briquetage. This is not to ignore continuing mining in Austria, now at the Dürrnberg rather than Hallstatt, however; and in Romania quarrying of rock salt using surface-dug shafts was certainly happening at one extensively excavated site (Băile Figa). We can presume that other places where salt rock outcrops on the earth's surface were also exploited in this way.

This Late Iron Age exploitation continued in most areas into the Roman period almost without a gap, though in some places the details of the briquetage technology changed somewhat. In many places, for instance in the Red Hills of eastern England, it is often hard to distinguish Late Iron Age from Roman period exploitation: the need for salt did not disappear, nor was there any pressing need for a successful technology to change. What almost certainly did change, however, at this transition as at others, was the role of salt in local and regional economies.

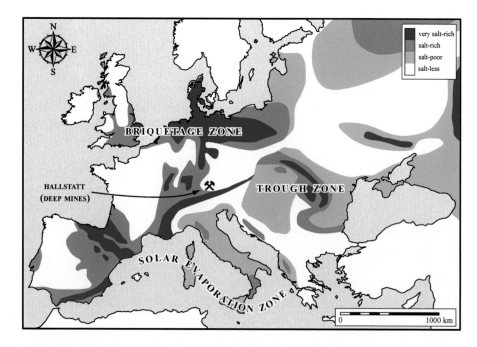

Fig. 7.1. The "salt zones" of Europe

The salt zones of Europe

In the light of the foregoing, it becomes possible to think of salt in European prehistory in a different way from what has previously been the situation. People in different areas, and at different times, produced salt in ways that were specific to them. While these were not hard and fast rules, they do lead towards a division of Europe into salt production "zones" (Fig. 7.1).

The best known is the *briquetage zone* (BZ), centred on eastern France and Germany, but extending to Britain in the west and Poland in the east; for the most part situated north of the Alps. In this zone solar evaporation would only have been possible in the middle of summer, perhaps for a couple of months (though not reliably so); at other times the sun would not have been hot enough for long enough for effective evaporation to take place, so boiling of brine over fires would be required: hence the need for containers of coarse ceramic, initially for boiling, later for drying and forming cakes or blocks.

South of the Alps and around the Mediterranean was the *solar evaporation zone* (SEZ). Here, by contrast, seawater or brine from springs could be evaporated between April and September, possibly longer. Crystalline salt could be collected from the edges of natural pans or lagoons, or from artificial pans of the sort still seen around Mediterranean shores today. This technique required a minimum of specialist equipment; pottery might be used to assist the process, but organic containers are just as likely.

In east-central Europe in the Bronze Age, and specifically in the Carpathian Basin, lay the *trough zone* (TZ), centred on Transylvania, but possibly extending beyond it to the east and north. As a part of temperate Europe, solar evaporation would only be possible for a few weeks each year; and local traditions apparently eschewed the use of ceramics for boiling brine after the Neolithic; why, we may well ask, since there was no lack of clay in the area, just as there was no lack of wood in the briquetage zone (or so it would appear). The fact that abundant briquetage has been found in Moldavia in the Neolithic shows, however, that these zones are not rigidly defined; traditions were capable of crossing zone boundaries.

In the Iron Age, the use of troughs seems to have been abandoned, though this is not completely certain. The troughs that have been dated all belong to the Bronze Age, but they were present, perhaps lying around, perhaps actually in use, in the Iron Age just as they are today, and it cannot be excluded that their use continued in parallel with surface mining or quarrying.

This leaves the mining areas of central and western Austria, represented primarily by Hallstatt and the Dürrnberg, outside any specific zone. Mining no doubt took place elsewhere where rock salt outcrops on the earth's surface, notably in Muntenia and Transylvania, but no archaeological trace of that exploitation survives, since such mining took place on the surface (and is thus better termed quarrying). The Austrian mines were intensively exploited, mainly during the Iron Age (early for Hallstatt, late for the Dürrnberg).

The zones as cross-cultural technologies

The three zones thus defined, BZ, SEZ and TZ, are a striking instance of cross-cultural technological convergence. While the SEZ is largely a result of environmental conditions, the other zones are culturally conditioned. In general one would expect the BZ to extend throughout temperate Europe, as indeed it did in its western half, regardless of which cultural groups were present in the area. The technology of brine-boiling was evidently deeply engrained in technological consciousness, though interestingly it started in the Neolithic in an area where it did not continue, and which was far from the regions where it later took strongest hold. Making coarse ceramic containers was not technically difficult; adjusting the variables in the boiling operation to achieve the desired end was more a matter of experimentation and acquired know-how than deep knowledge. On the other hand, the technology needed for the trough technique (in the TZ), as for deep mining, was highly specialised. It was presumably also successful in achieving its ends. Why then did it not continue into the Iron Age and beyond? Equally puzzling, why was it adopted at all, when everybody else at the time was using an evaporation technique, or mining?

The three zonal techniques were thus non-specific in cultural terms; the technologies can truly be regarded as cross-cultural in a way that pottery-making was not, and bronze-smithing only to a certain degree. True, the pyrotechnological processes involved in these crafts were known everywhere, but the outcomes were highly variable; not so with salt-making. In this, salt was a true pan-European phenomenon.

Chapter 8

Salt as an economic resource

The consideration of salt production undertaken so far in this work has principally concerned ancient technology: how, when and where salt was produced. At this point the investigation will take a different path, looking instead at how salt might have been integrated into the prehistoric economy. To the individual, and thus to groups of individuals ("groups", "societies" etc), salt was a substance that had an immediate impact on everyday life, since it was probably consumed and used every day. But to economic organisations, or social organisations that also served an economic role, salt was important for other reasons and raises a different set of questions: how it was distributed, what its value was, and how those in salt-poor regions obtained it from the source areas. Salt as a substance became a commodity during prehistory (see below, chapter 9) and thus was only one of a number of materials that formed part of the prehistoric economy. We need to consider the extent to which it can be correlated with these other materials, and to what extent it went its own way; one specific relationship to assess is that with bronze hoards deposited in the Bronze Age.

The scale of production

As discussed above, the scale of Iron Age production using briquetage was on a completely different scale from that seen in the Bronze Age. The great batteries of flues and furnaces recovered in the Seille valley, and the tonnes of briquetage, can only mean production on an industrial scale. By comparison, the Bronze Age briquetage sites around Halle bespeak regular but not large-scale production, since each site is restricted in extent. For Hallstatt, the quantities involved cannot be known in detail, but it is clear that there were more mines in operation in the Iron Age than the Bronze Age, and since the latter lasted longer than the former it is reasonable to suppose that Iron Age production was much larger than Bronze Age production. But in none of these cases is it known in what form the salt obtained was transported. Hallstatt itself has provided a large amount of organic material for carrying salt around the site, in textile, leather and wood (Kern *et al.* 2009: 60-61, 102-5), so such containers may well have been used for further transportation as well. This is speculative, but reasonable speculation.

With coastal lagoons we are again in the realm of speculation, but since it is known that coastal Italy supplied the needs of Rome (and presumably its many other large cities as well) one must suppose that production was on a large scale. In such situations one would not expect to find specific archaeological evidence, any more than today's installations require much more than buildings to store the salt.

The sites that used the trough technique, however, provide good evidence for extensive production capabilities. I have discussed in Chapter 5 the potential of the Romanian trough sites in this respect. While one would hesitate to call these sites industrial, the scale of production seems to have been extensive and long-lived.

Valeriu Cavruc and I have considered how different production techniques might have been used in prehistoric times, and led to different end-users of the product (Cavruc & Harding 2012). In this analysis, we distinguished between domestic, industrial and sacred salt production, suggesting the parameters one might expect for each type. Thus domestic production should take place close to the settlement, use quite simple technology, process the product minimally, and produce relatively small quantities for household consumption. By contrast, industrial production would take place wherever major salt sources were available (sometimes at considerable distances from settlement), producing high quality salt in large quantities, destined principally for exchange. Finally, ritual or sacred salt production would aim to produce very high quality salt, using specialised technology and much processing; the product would be intended for specialist use, probably at some distance from the place of production, and the quantity produced might be quite small.

These are theoretical notions of production; the task remains to consider how they might relate to the archaeological evidence. In the absence of clear indications of how the process operated there is some guesswork involved here, but we maintain that most production using briquetage, prior to the Iron Age, was domestic in character, and small in scale. Briquetage production in the Iron Age was, by contrast on a large scale and presumably industrial in nature. Mining at Hallstatt and the Dürrnberg, and production by the trough technique, was also arguably industrial in scale. It is not clear which archaeological manifestation, if any, might relate to "sacred" production, nor does this materially affect the outcomes.

The movement of salt

It is not in doubt that salt was moved between different parts of prehistoric Europe: as discussed in Chapter 1, the need of individuals and communities for salt meant that those without it had to get hold of supplies of it. The question is, how did it move and on what scale?

In this context, the contributions of ethnography may be relevant, since the salt trade has been extensively recorded in modern times, particularly in north Africa, where salt cakes were moved over large distances.

Godelier (1969) described the process of production and distribution of salt among the Baruja of New Guinea. The different "salt lands" were appropriated by various lineages, who may or may not have allowed others to use them. Specific rules or customs were followed in the exchange process: of fifteen cakes or bars produced, five to ten might be exchanged, the others left for domestic use. Others might be destined for particular people, including the sorcerer and the salt-maker.

Fig. 8.1. Caravan moving cakes of salt in North Africa (source: Edwardje, Dreamstime.com)

The going rate for exchange with those outside the group varied according to status, and most exchanges took place within a range of 50 km or three days walk. Salt served as a medium of value, in Godelier's opinion as a kind of primitive money.

There is extensive evidence from central and southern Africa for the importance of salt in local and regional economies. Graham Connah, for instance, has shown how important it has been in the economy of Kibiro (Uganda) (Connah 1991). In Botswana, expeditions of not more than ten people would go to collect salt from the various pans. Though the details differ from area to area, in one, dried blocks of salt would be bound together to go on a donkey's back, and then be taken to a district where it could be exchanged for sorghum or other goods (Matshetshe 2001).

In Mexico, Good has described how caravans of 20-25 burros (small donkeys) or mules and 10-12 men would set off from the inland valley of Balsas to the coast during the hottest time of year, 150 km distant through mountainous terrain, the outward journey taking seven days and the return eight, leaving food en route at prearranged spots and travelling by night when possible (Good 1995). Kinship networks were important for forming the caravans and providing the manpower. The salt thus obtained would be sold for several times its price on the coast, making the journey worthwhile. Although each caravan was formed from small kinship units, in total the trade was highly active, with large numbers of mule-trains arriving at the saltworks, obtaining their salt, and immediately setting off again.

It is from north Africa, however, that the most abundant evidence for the salt trade comes: Mali, Niger, Mauritania, Sudan and Ethiopia have all seen extensive use of salt in trade (Lovejoy 1986; Nave 2010)(Fig. 8.1). The prolific mines at Taghaza and Taoudenni in northern Mali were an important part of the wealth of

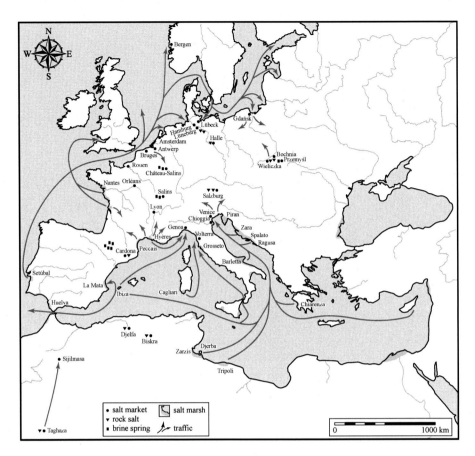

Fig. 8.2. The international trade in salt in Europe in the 15th century, according to Michel Mollat (1968)

the medieval Mali empire (Insoll 2000). There are many accounts in the literature of the camel caravans that brought the mined blocks of salt from these sources south to Timbuktu and Gao, and thence along the Niger river to the sea, or north to Marrakesh and the Mediterranean. Given that the Taoudenni Basin lies in one of the hottest places on earth, in mid-Sahara, the very existence of the mines and the salt trade is remarkable, let alone its scale.

In the context of prehistoric Europe, little is known for sure about how salt moved or in what form – the consequence of its solubility and perhaps too of the nature of the containers, if any, in which it was moved. But it is possible to make some educated guesses about the situation, based on the assumed scale of production in various contexts. Here it is useful to make a distinction between the Iron Age and earlier periods; and between techniques relying on evaporation (salt lagoons and briquetage) and those relying on other methods, notably mining and/or the trough technique.

In determining how and along what routes salt was transported, several lines of investigation might be followed. None of them directly involves salt itself, for the reasons outlined above. Some have argued that trade routes can be detected

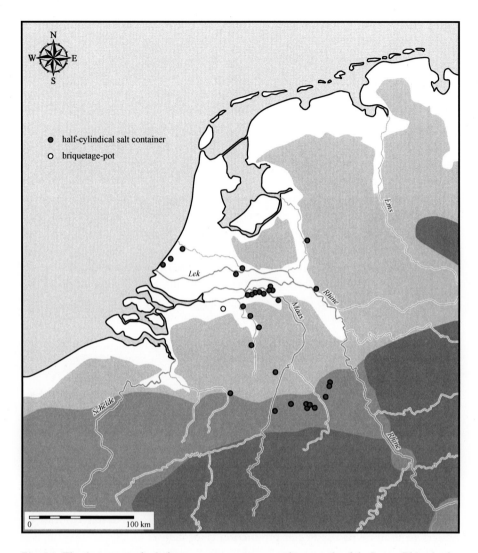

Fig. 8.3. The movement of salt from source to consumer: the example of the Lower Rhine in the Iron Age (source: P. van den Broeke)

through the location of archaeological sites and finds, for instance along waterways; this was the method by which Ernst Sprockhoff suggested a network of interlinked nodes for the Brandenburg and Mecklenburg regions of Germany in the Bronze Age (Sprockhoff 1930: 145 Taf. 45). Others have made use of known historical or ethnographic trade routes. Nicolaus Olahus, for instance, archbishop of Esztergom in the 16th century, refers to the transport of salt from Transylvania along the rivers Someş/Szamos, Mureş/Maros and Tisza into central Hungary (Marc 2006: 153). Doina Ciobanu has discussed the question of salt production and trade in the Carpatho-Danubian area in the early Middle Ages, giving many comparable examples (Ciobanu 2006). Virginia Rau did the same for Portugal (1968) and many other authors have considered the medieval and early modern salt trade.

Fig. 8.2 shows the international salt trade in the 15th century according to Michel Mollat (1968: map on p. 335), who also gave a general overview of the situation in Europe (ibid. 11 ff.). As Mollat pointed out (ibid. 17), salt is a bulk commodity that is heavy and burdensome, and only worth transporting in large volumes – at least in the historical period. These might have consisted either of many small boats or a few large ones (Genoese or Hanseatic in the period he was discussing). Salt was transported by sea, along rivers, and (less commonly) over land; the reconstruction which has been suggested both for northern Germany by Sprockhoff, and by Kavruk and Harding for Romania, suggests riverine routes as the most likely in prehistory.

Archaeological examples suggest that the movement of salt may indeed be traced through the distribution of pottery containers in which it was moved. This is the case for the products of the Droitwich and Cheshire sources in Iron Age England, for example (Morris 1985; 1994); for the movement of North Sea salt to the Lower Rhine area (van den Broeke 1995) (Fig. 8.3); and from Channel coasts to inland France (Prilaux 2000: 95-6, Fig. 59; Prilaux *et al.* 2011). Equally one may suppose that the finds of briquetage in Lausitz culture graves during the Late Bronze Age, or on settlements well away from proven production zones, must show a movement of salt in clay containers.

Analytical methods

One of the ways in which the movement of salt might be detected would be through the detection of salt residues from specific sources on pottery. There have been few attempts at such analysis, mainly because salt is so soluble that it has been considered unlikely to leave identifiable residues. Flad and colleagues showed that salt residues on suspected briquetage concentrate on the inside of the vessel, and are undetectable after around 2 mm from the inside surface (1 mm in the case of chlorine); hardly encouraging for the detection of residues at non-production sites (Flad *et al.* 2005). Horiuchi and colleagues attempted to detect chloride on pottery to indicate its use in salt production (Horiuchi *et al.* 2011); they suggest that chloride ions may be captured within the pottery matrix and bound within it, either strongly or weakly. They thus developed a method for extracting the strongly bound chloride ions, and were able to show that this chloride does indeed remain in pottery that had been used for salt boiling. This only shows, however, what pottery has been used for salt production and what has not; it does not distinguish between different salt sources.

To get round this difficulty, a set of analyses was designed by Jens Andersen of the Camborne School of Mines, in which both ICP-MS and electron microprobe analysis would be used on salt samples (brine, crystals, and rock salt) and pottery from salt-production sites. ICP-MS was able to show that there were significant differences between the samples from the different sites; and there was also significant difference between the brines and the rock salt, probably because of fractionation effects. Microprobe analysis did indeed confirm that the pottery has salt on the sherd surface in the form of sodium and chlorine; it also showed that sherds collected from a site a few kilometres away, suggested as a salt trading station, have no detectable salt in them – not necessarily proving that the site was unconnected with salt, but not disproving the idea either. Finally, the sherds had surface salts removed and were ground up and re-analysed using ICP-MS. Unfortunately this did not succeed in separating the sherds from different salt sources; for this it is anticipated that isotopic techniques will be needed.

The field thus remains open for further analytical work which will provide solutions to the question of the transport of salt in pottery containers.

Salt and metal

In general there is not much overlap between salt sources and non-ferrous metal sources; not surprising, given the different geologies that are involved. Obvious exceptions are certain mountain regions, notably the Alps, and parts of Transylvania. Boroffka (2006; 2009) (Fig. 8.4) has shown how in the latter region all these minerals appear in close proximity – which is not to say, however, that their exploitation was interlinked except in terms of extraction technology. The appearance of waisted hammers (German *Rillenhämmer*, sometimes called "mining tools" in English) in both copper extraction areas and salt mining sites indicates that similar processes were involved in both types of mine. But in terms of products, there is no obvious reason why salt and metals should be linked.

There is a notable exception to this statement, however. For many years it has been stated in the literature that the bronze hoards deposited in the Bronze Age were most frequent in areas where salt sources are present, and specifically that the very large hoards that sometimes occur – where tens or even hundreds of kilograms of metal are present – were a consequence of the nearby presence of rich salt deposits. This has been stated particularly for Romania, rich in salt and home to many hoards, including some very large ones, but if it was true for Romania, presumably it could equally well have been true for other areas.

Mircea Rusu was one of the first to make this connection, originally in the 1960s and repeated later (Rusu 1963; 1981). Rusu saw the mechanism quite simply as a straightforward exchange of metal and salt, leading to an "enrichment" not only of communities as a whole, but also of those at the top of society, part of the so-

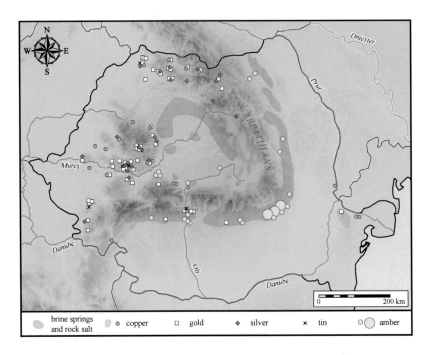

Fig. 8.4. The sources of raw materials in Romania (source: N. Boroffka)

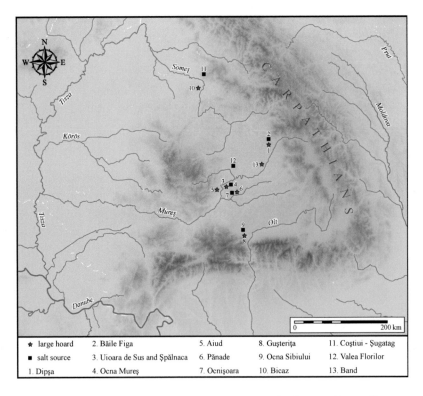

Fig. 8.5. The association between large bronze hoards and salt, according to H. Ciugudean (2006)

called "gentile aristocracy" so beloved of Marxist historians going back to Engels.[28] Wollmann (1996: 408) repeated the theory without elaboration. More recently Horia Ciugudean has reiterated and amplified the point, though the mechanism remains much the same as for Rusu (Ciugudean 2012; Ciugudean *et al.* 2006). (Fig. 8.5) A similar argument was made for Maramureş by Carol Kacsó (2009), though for the most part this author restricted himself to pointing out that there are some 60 bronze hoards in the region, including that from Bogdan Vodă with more than 230 objects, the Maramureş being home to some very important salt deposits such as those at Ocna Şugatag and Coştiui.

Something similar has been suggested for Bronze Age France (Carozza *et al.* 2009: 52), but not yet worked out in detail. Certainly salt has been associated with rhythmical cycles of change, of increase and decrease in population numbers and environmental impact (Pétrequin & Weller 2007); access to and production of bronze would of course be part of that impact.

The idea is that those who controlled the production and distribution of salt would have been able to acquire "wealth" in the form of abundant metal; much the same mechanism as used to be alleged for the Wessex culture of southern England (control of the gold trade from Ireland) or the Early Iron Age cemetery at Hallstatt (control of the salt, as suggested both for Hallstatt and for the rich graves at the cemetery of Helpfau-Uttendorf in Upper Austria: Egg 1985). Nico Roymans has suggested that the development of prestige burials in Ha C in the Netherlands owes much to control of salt from the North Sea going to communities in the Upper Rhenish area (Roymans 1991: 51 ff.). These ideas seem superficially attractive, though it is not clear how this mechanism might actually have worked in practice; they have been challenged on other grounds too, by van den Broeke (in Louwe Kooijmans *et al.* 2005), since the evidence suggests that production on the North Sea was relatively modest in scale, and high-status individuals may have been connected to wide-ranging networks that could have brought salt from the German or Alpine sources.

---

28 "Um die Gründe zu erklären, die die Verbergung der Horte der Gruppe Uriu-Domăneşti bestimmten, ist in erster Linie an innere Faktoren zu denken ... doch dürfen auch die auswärtigen Faktoren nicht ausser Acht gelassen werden ... Die wiederholten Zusammenstösse zwischen den Stämmen der Kulturen von Wietenberg, Noua, Otomani und Suciu de Sus, in ihrem Kampf um Acker- und Weideland oder um das für Mensch und Vieh nötige *Salz*, sind die Hauptgründe für die Verbergung dieser Horte.... Die eindrucksvolle Menge an transsilvanischen Bronzefunden aus der Hallstattstufe A 1 ist einerseits auf die stärkere Ausbeutung der Gold-, Kupfer- und Salzvorkommen, demnach also auf die Zunahme der Produktionskräfte, andererseits auf den beträchtlichen Bevölkerungszuwachs zurückzuführen, der durch die grosse Zahl der Siedlungen dieser Zeit verdeutlicht wird. Hierzu kommt noch die Ausweitung und Intensivierung der Wirtschaftsbeziehungen, ist es doch sicherlich kein Zufall, dass die erwähnten grossen Horte [Uioara, Şpălnaca, Guşteriţa, Dipşa, Band] in unmittelbarer Nähe von Salzlagern auftreten. Der Tauschverkehr mit der wertvollen Bronze und dem so nötigen and viel begehrten Salz führte zur Bereicherung nicht nur der Stammesgemeinschaften, sondern auch der Spitzen der in voller Entwicklung begriffenen Gentilaristokratie" (Rusu 1963: 183-4). "In unmittelbaren Nähe von den genannten und auch anderen Salzvorkommen wurden Bronzehorte, Goldschätze, Niederlassungen und Burgen der Stufe Ha A1 entdeckt, so dass ihre Ausbeutung zu jener Zeit fast als sicher angenommen werden muss. Im Tausch bekam man für die Salzklumpen bedeutende Mengen von Metallen in verschiedenen Formen: Fertigwaren oder Bruchstücke, Gussfladen, Barren, was die Anlage und das Wachstum von grossen Werkstätten zur Bronzeverarbeitung in unmittelbarer Nähe der Salinen förderte" (Rusu 1981: 382).

The trouble with assumptions of association like these is that they rely on a purely impressionistic idea of relationships between two phenomena. While it is true that there are large bronze hoards in areas that contain salt resources, to show that one depended on the other requires a much more detailed analysis. In part this is a result of local scholars working with local material and ignoring the wider picture: Romania is not the only country where large hoards turn up. Presumably the authors would not suggest that salt was the only, or even the main, cause of their deposition across Europe.

In Britain, for instance, the hoard from Isleham, Cambridgeshire, contains more than 6500 pieces and weighs over 90 kg (Britton 1960); in France, the hoard from Villethierry (Yonne) contained 913 pieces (Mordant *et al.* 1976); that from Vénat (St-Yrieix, Charente) some 75 kg of metal with 2720 pieces, 802 intact (Coffyn *et al.* 1981: 17); that from Petit-Villatte (Neuvy-sur-Barangeon, Cher) 628 pieces (Coffyn *et al.* 1981; Cordier 2009; Cordier & Bourhis 1996); and that from Larnaud (Jura) with 1815 pieces (Coffyn *et al.* 1981: 36-40, for a discussion of large hoards in France; Coutil 1913). There is no reason to suppose that any of these has any connection with salt; indeed, since they all appear in the late decades of the Bronze Age, other explanations have been suggested (such as dumping of bronze as iron came into use – though this is not in fact the likeliest explanation).

Nor should possible relationships of salt with other phenomena be ignored; for instance with metal sources, in which Romania is also very rich, particularly in the Munţii Metalici in western Transylvania. It would indeed seem perfectly reasonable that there should be a close relationship between abundant metal products and the sources from which the metal came. Of course metals were moved around extensively in the Bronze Age, so this is far from guaranteed. One has only to think of the situation with tin, whose sources in Europe are very limited and which must have travelled considerable distances on a regular basis – as is indeed clear from the finding of tin ingots in a probable cargo in the sea off Salcombe, Devon, south-west England (not yet published; see e.g. http://www.artfund.org/what-we-do/art-weve-helped-buy/artwork/11559/salcombe-hoard, accessed 25 July 2013). Nevertheless, while one can certainly argue that the abundant hoards of north-east Hungary were made of Transylvanian copper, it would be foolish to suppose that this was their only source or that their existence depended on the copper sources 250 km to their south-east.

In order to investigate these matters further, we have conducted a GIS-based analysis of the locations of bronze hoards and salt sources in the eastern half of Europe.[29] The areas involved are those where information is available on both salt sources and bronze hoards. There are some obvious difficulties here, mostly relating to the completeness of the datasets involved. The two variables, salt and hoards, are different in nature: while salt sources are generally known about, and what is present today must also have been present in prehistory, the bronze hoards are only

---

29   I am grateful to Dr Chris Smart who carried out the analyses, and to the Leverhulme Trust for supporting the work.

those that have survived the various processes of deposition and post-depositional history (original presence and survival). In placing salt sources on the map, we have to consider to what extent people with prehistoric technology would have been able to exploit the resource; it is also likely that springs have moved position – though they necessarily reflect the presence of a salt massif underground, which has obviously *not* moved. Similarly, the precise findspot of many hoards is not known, only an area (sometimes a field name or grid reference is recorded, more often the commune, or frequently a larger area still). So it can never be a *precise* proximity that is supposed to have existed, only a *general* one, as Ciugudean's maps bear out.

In spite of these difficulties, we mapped the available data, as follows:

Salt sources:

Western Ukraine: information from pre-World War II Polish sources (Windakiewicz 1926: 105-7, with map), and from Josip Kobal' (Uzhgorod)

Poland: information from Czapowski and Bukowski (2009; 2010), based on earlier sources (Szajnocha 1891; 1893; Windakiewicz 1926), with additions

Slovakia: information from Dr Eva Horvathová (Archaeological Institute, Košice)

Romania: information from Ciobanu (2002), based on Stoica & Gherasie (1981) and Drăgănescu (1997)

Information for Austria, Croatia, Bosnia etc based on internet sources

There are no salt deposits in present-day Hungary (references on the internet to Hungarian salt all refer to pre-1920 Hungary).

Hoards:

The main source has been the book of Olimpia Bratu (2009), which is based on the principal publications up until that time; these cover Romania, Moldova, Transcarpathian Ukraine, Hungary, Slovakia, Croatia, Serbia, Slovenia, Bosnia-Herzegovina, and Bulgaria (I do not include the references for these, which can be found in Bratu's book). For some areas the lists of Svend Hansen (1994) have been used.

Other areas are:

Western Ukraine (Precarpathia) (Kobal' 1992; Żurowski 1949 [1950]), with additional information from Wojciech Blajer (Kraków) and Josip Kobal' (Uzhgorod)

Bohemia (Kytlicová 2007)

Moravia (Salaš 2005)

Poland (Blajer 2001)

Austria (Hansen 1994; Lauermann & Rammer 2013)

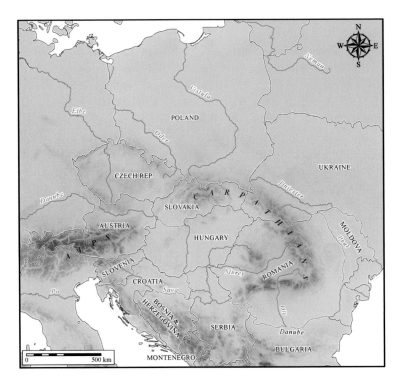

Fig. 8.6. Map of central and eastern Europe, showing the areas investigated

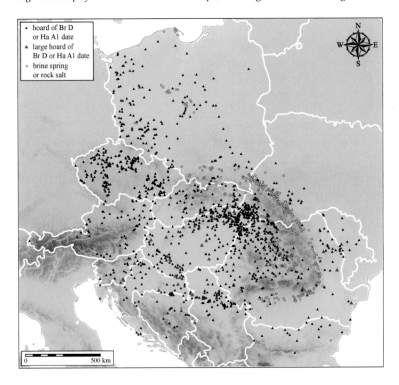

Fig. 8.7. Distribution of hoards of Br D and Ha A1, and of salt sources (rock salt or brine springs). For the source of the information see text.

It must be noted that the analysis covers the area from Austria in the west as far as Romania and Moldova in the east, along with the westernmost part of Ukraine, and takes in Poland, the Czech and Slovak Republics, Hungary, and the countries of former Yugoslavia. No mapping has been done for Italy or Germany (Fig. 8.6).

The period when the largest number of hoards was deposited in central and eastern Europe was Ha A1. This equates to, for instance, the Cincu-Suseni horizon in Romania, the Aranyos and Kurd horizons in Hungary, hoard horizon II in Serbia and Croatia, Martinček-Bodrog in Slovakia, and Suchdol in the Czech Republic. It was the time when the very large hoards in Transylvania were deposited (Uioara de Sus, Gușterița II, Dipșa etc). In most countries there was a notable fall-off in the succeeding periods. However, the sources did not always differentiate the internal divisions of Ha A, especially in "outlying" regions such as Ukraine, so some finds have been included which do not fall within the strict definition of Ha A1 as opposed to adjacent periods. We have also considered the situation with Br D, which, while not as prolific in hoards as Ha A1, has a considerable number and merges imperceptibly with Ha A1.

The procedure followed has been to create spatially correct point datasets for the location of hoards, rock salt deposits and brine springs, and polygon datasets for salt-bearing geological zones in ESRI ArcGIS (Fig. 8.7). The accuracy of the resultant point and polygon datasets is dependent on that of the original source. Sites were derived either from maps – these were taken from published sources and georeferenced – or from gazetteers – in which case places were located on digital base mapping. There are two caveats concerning the degree of precision: some distribution maps were not fine-grained in the detail of country boundaries or rivers – the types of common features by which one would georeference a raster image – so total correlation could often not be achieved; sites recorded in gazetteers only gave a place-name and not a precise latitude/longitude or equivalent local grid reference, so points were entered in the dataset based on the location of that place, or the centre of the local district (e.g. commune (*comună, Gemeinde* etc), district (*okres, Kreis, Bezirk, raion* etc) even county (*județ, kraj, oblast* etc) where no better information is available). A cross check of accuracy between georeferenced distribution maps and gazetteer entries, for example the brine spring sites in south-west Ukraine, suggested that there was rarely more than 1-2 km difference (often much less) in the position of a site achieved using either method. Given the parameters of the quantitative analysis this is quite satisfactory.

The objective of this analysis – that we should test over a wide area the spatial relationship between bronze hoards and salt resources – was easily achieved using the proximity analysis function of ArcGIS, specifically the "near" calculation tool. This facility enables the closest distance between points or areas in one dataset (e.g. bronze hoards) and a second dataset (e.g. salt sources) to be automatically calculated. The trend of these proximity values is best demonstrated in standard chart form.

The results

The relative densities of Br D and Ha A1 hoards were mapped (Fig. 8.8), as was that of salt sources (Fig. 8.9) and copper and gold sources (Fig. 8.10). The relative density of hoards was mapped against that of brine springs and sources of rock salt (Fig. 8.11) and against copper and gold sources (Fig. 8.12). This was done for each dataset using the density calculation function of the Spatial Analyst toolset in ArcGIS. Kernel density estimation was used to model the density of these variables, producing a smoothed calculation of magnitude (in our case the number of hoards or salt sources) per unit area. This non-parametric estimator takes into account the entire group for each class of point data, and provides a more refined means of representing the spatial distribution of a dataset than, for example, a standard histogram (e.g. Silverman 1998). The graduations within the raster density models for hoards and salt were established using the Jenks Natural Breaks classification, which groups values to optimise the variance between classes. At this stage, relative densities have been qualitatively compared, not quantitatively.

Following this, graphs were produced showing the proximity of hoards to salt and to copper and gold in various subsets of the region studied. From the graph for all hoards over the entire area (Fig. 8.13), it is clear that there is no special association between hoards and salt sources. The cumulative percentage graph shows a steady increase in hoard numbers with distance. There is, however, a slightly increased tendency for large hoards (those with more than 20 kg of metal or 100 pieces, excluding small ornaments) to congregate within 50 km of salt sources when compared to standard hoards. The same pattern is evident when considering the Carpathian Basin on its own (Fig. 8.14). For the subset of the Carpathian Basin that is Transylvania (which is where the association with salt has been asserted), there is a closer link between all hoards and large hoards (Fig. 8.15); "standard" hoards are actually slightly more likely to occur within 5 km of a salt source than are "large" hoards, though this pattern is reversed at all other distances up to 30 km. At that distance, all large hoards are included.

These figures appear to offer some justification to the oft-repeated assertion of an association between hoards, and specifically large hoards, and salt. A number of caveats must be entered, however. First, the precise location of hoards is often not recorded, as discussed above. Second, this is not a pan-European phenomenon; it is specific to Transylvania. Third, in an area like Transylvania, much of which lies over salt massifs, almost any spot is likely to be close to some sort of salt source, either rock or spring . One might imagine that proximity to copper sources would be just as important (Fig. 8.16), though in fact no such trend is visible.

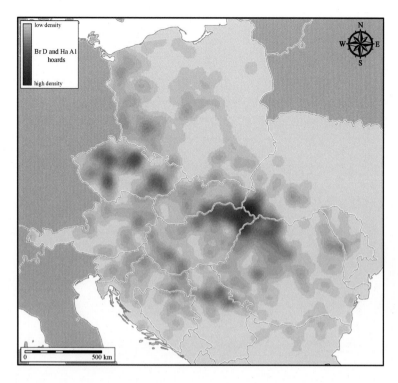

Fig. 8.8. Bronze hoards of Br D and Ha A1: density estimate

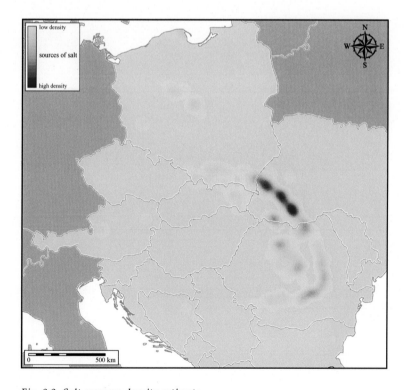

Fig. 8.9. Salt sources: density estimate

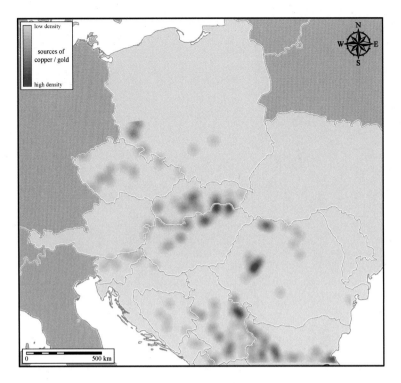

Fig. 8.10. Copper and gold sources: density estimate

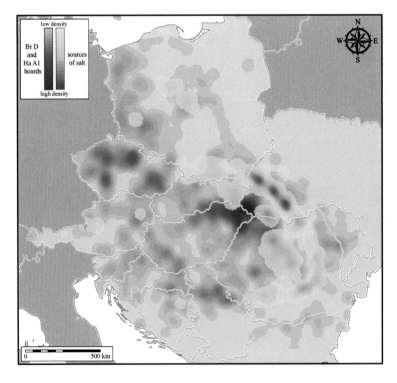

Fig. 8.11. Hoards of Br D / Ha A1 and salt sources: density estimate

SALT IN PREHISTORIC EUROPE

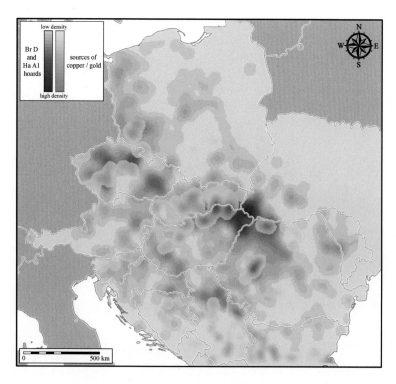

Fig. 8.12. Hoards of Br D / Ha A1 and copper & gold sources: density estimate

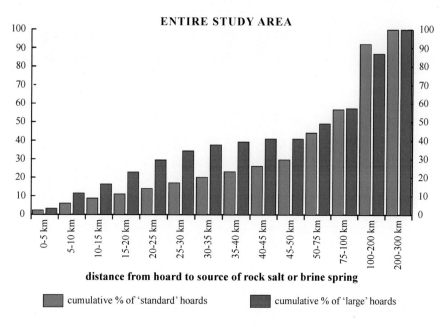

Fig. 8.13. The distance of "standard" and "large" hoards from salt sources in the entire study area. The blue lines and bars represent "standard" hoards and show a regular fall-off pattern with distance from salt source (no evident correlation). The red lines and bars represent the smaller number of "large" hoards (as defined in the text) and, whilst also having a regular fall-off pattern, show a slightly increased tendency to congregate within 50 km of a salt source.

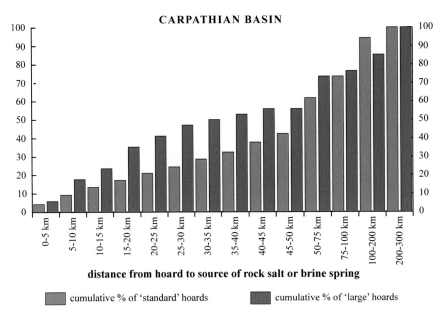

Fig. 8.14. The distance of "standard" and "large" hoards from salt sources in the Carpathian Basin. Blue: "standard" hoards, red: "large" hoards. The graphs show similar fall-off patterns for "standard" and "large" hoards to those for the entire study area.

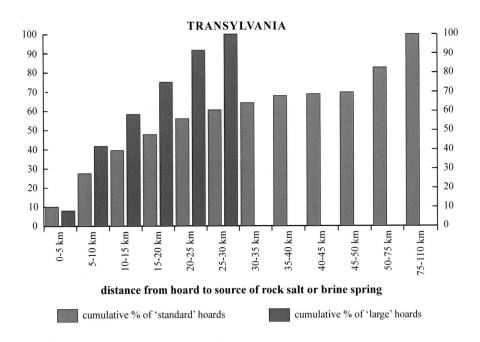

Fig. 8.15. The distance of "standard" and "large" hoards from salt sources in Transylvania. Blue: "standard" hoards, red: "large" hoards. The graphs show an obvious trend for large hoards to be situated nearer salt sources than do standard hoards.

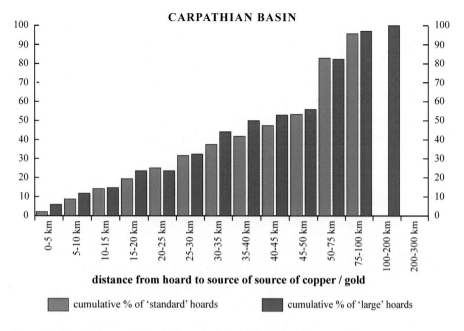

CARPATHIAN BASIN

distance from hoard to source of source of copper / gold

☐ cumulative % of 'standard' hoards   ■ cumulative % of 'large' hoards

Fig. 8.16. The distance of "standard" and "large" hoards from copper and gold sources in the Carpathian Basin. For both a regular fall-off with distance is apparent.

Perhaps most important, we must consider the reasons why hoards in general, and large hoards in particular, might have been deposited, both in Europe as a whole and specifically in Transylvania. This is not the place to enter into a full discussion of a much-debated topic, other than to reiterate the widely held view at the present day that hoards were seldom, if ever, deposited for utilitarian reasons. Though the idea of "ritual" deposition does not appeal to every palate, it is the only explanation which can account satisfactorily for all or almost all hoards; and in this, Transylvania was no different from any other part of Europe. Those who wish to press for a connection between hoard deposition and abundance of salt or any other natural resource need to come up with a satisfactory mechanism by which this occurred, in social and in economic terms. Merely stating that "salt brought wealth" is not enough; if it were, why did it not do so in other salt-rich areas as well? Conversely, why was metal wealth often far removed from salt sources?

One way in which progress might be made in understanding correlations between hoards and other phenomena might be to look at areas where there are many hoards and no evidence of salt production. Such an area is present-day Hungary, especially its north-eastern part, though this area has already been included in the analysis described above, the rich salt sources of Transylvania and Maramureş lying only a few score kilometres to the east. One could argue that these sources, even if not in the immediate vicinity, nevertheless influenced the ability of communities to acquire metal wealth. The Sava corridor in northern Croatia also fulfils these requirements, and here there is no salt within several hundred kilometres. The large hoards of Brodski Varoš, Podcrkavlje-Slavonski Brod, or Otok-Privlaka all lie in this area (Vinski-Gasparini 1973). Or one could look at an area such as

Denmark, where there are many hoards (Levy 1982) but no salt production other than possible seawater evaporation (cf Jaanusson & Jaanusson 1988). It would be far-fetched indeed to see a connection between the two phenomena there.

The conclusion of this analysis must be that while a specific correlation between very large hoards in Transylvania and the presence of major salt sources cannot be ruled out, in general the distribution of hoards – including large ones in other parts of Europe – does little to support the idea. The question should more accurately be considered part of the wider issue surrounding hoard deposition in general.

Salt as an economic resource: conclusion

Since salt was a necessity of life, and not everyone had immediate access to it, it had to be procured, extracted, and transported. In this respect, it was an economic resource like any other. How it was transported, and along what routes, are matters of speculation for prehistory, though good indicators are present in historical and ethnographic sources. On the other hand, the analyses discussed above show a very limited likelihood that bronze hoards of the Bronze Age were located where they are simply because of the nearby presence of abundant salt sources. Certainly hoards in general do not exhibit any such pattern.

The chances of discovery may yet yield vestiges of salt on the move, in the form of the containers in which they were transported. To date, attempts at identifying the unique signature of specific salt sources on pottery have not been successful, but future research may yet unlock the enormous potential of that data source. If and when that happens, the scene will be set for a transformation of our knowledge of the role of salt in the prehistoric economy.

Chapter 9

Salt and society

In the preceding chapters I have sketched how salt was produced in Europe from earliest times down to the Roman period. Most of this information relates to the technology involved, and to the areas and places where the production took place. It has had very little to say about the position of salt production in the communities involved, let alone the individuals who took part in the production. But this remains, in essence, the most important aspect of the study of ancient salt. Salt was produced for human needs (which includes the fact that animals also need salt); so the context in which it was produced is of great importance. Who did the work at the salt mines, lagoons, marshes, or springs? Was it a domestic enterprise, or an industrial one, or something in between? Were the various tasks carried out by men, women, or children? What were the processes – mental or physical – which had to be gone through in order to produce salt? These are questions which directly bear on our understanding of the societies which were producing salt, even though the answers to most of them must remain speculative.

Pliny the Elder's remarks indicate something of the value that attached to salt in the Roman world; we may assume that what went for the Romans of the first century AD probably applied to other Mediterranean peoples, to centuries before his, and in many aspects to those who lived in the Roman empire beyond the Mediterranean:

> *To season meats and foods the most useful [salt] melts easily and is rather moist, for it is less bitter, such as that of Attica and Euboea. For preserving meat the more suitable salt is sharp and dry, like that of Megara. A conserve too is made with fragrant additions, which is used as a relish, creating and sharpening an appetite for every kind of food, so that in innumerable seasonings it is the taste of salt that predominates, and it is looked for when we eat garum. Moreover sheep, cattle, and draught animals are encouraged to pasture in particular by salt; the supply of milk is much more copious, and there is even a far more pleasing quality in the cheese.*

Therefore, by Hercules, a civilized life is impossible without salt, and so necessary is this basic substance that its name is applied metaphorically even to intense mental pleasures. We call them sales (wit); all the humour of life, its supreme joyousness, and relaxation after toil, are expressed by this word more than by any other (Natural History Book 31: 87-88; Loeb translation, slightly adapted)[30]

So it is evident here that in the Roman period salt was generally regarded as not only a necessity of life in terms of health, but also of pleasure in eating, giving its name metaphorically to sharpness of intellect, wit, or intelligence generally.

An obvious parallel can be seen in the biblical Sermon on the Mount (Matthew 5:13): "Ye are the salt of the earth: but if the salt have lost his savour, wherewith shall it be salted? it is thenceforth good for nothing, but to be cast out, and to be trodden under foot of men". Jesus was presumably referring to the preservative and purifying qualities of salt, meaning that the disciples would preserve and purify human souls, but the expression thereafter took on a different meaning: as a metaphor "salt of the earth" represents honest and worthy people, and reappears in literature so often as to have become part of everyday speech. Among the many uses that have followed, Chaucer's "Ye been the salt of the erthe and the savour" in the Summoner's Tale (line 2196) is one of the first in English; the phrase has inspired a 1970s Austrian TV series and a pop song by Sting.

But in spite of the importance of salt for people in the ancient world, and despite the fact that many aspects of the technology of its production have become clearer in recent years, there are many things that have been little investigated about salt and its role in ancient (particularly prehistoric) life.

Chaînes opératoires

Making salt in prehistory was a technological process, involving a *chaîne opératoire* or sequence of actions. The notion of the *chaîne opératoire* is now commonplace in archaeology. Originally applied to the process of stone tool making, in more recent years it has frequently been applied to potting as well as other technical processes (e.g. Roux 2010; van der Leeuw 1993); salt-making is in this light no different, since a series of actions had to be gone through in order to produce the end product, salt.

"Any technique, in any society... be it mere gesture or a simple artefact, is always the physical rendering of mental schemas learned through tradition and concerned with how things work, are to be made, and to be used... Some of these are related

---

30 87 ad opsonium et cibum utilior quisquis facile liquescit, item umidior, minorem enim amaritudinem habent, ut Atticus et Euboicus. servandis carnibus aptior acer et siccus, ut Megaricus. conditur etiam odoribus additis et pulmentarii vicem implet, excitans aviditatem invitansque in omnibus cibis ita, ut sit peculiaris ex eo intellectus inter innumera condimenta ciborum item in mandendo quaesitus garo. quin et pecudes armentaque et iumenta sale maxime sollicitantur ad pastus multum largiore lacte multoque gratiore etiam in caseo dote.

88 ergo, Hercules, vita humanior sine sale non quit degere, adeoque necessarium elementum est uti transierit intellectus ad voluptates animi quoque nimias. sales appellantur, omnisque vitae lepos et summa hilaritas laborumque requies non alio magis vocabulo constat.

to the basic, universal, and necessary principles of action or to the physical laws involved in action on matter... Others are mental algorithms or a mental planning of the sequence of operations involved in a given task" (Lemonnier 1993: 3).

The creation of these techniques, principles of action or mental algorithms is based on learning: learning through tradition, through apprenticeship, through generational handing down; the acquisition of motor skills and the creation of cognitive processes, which mean that the novice can, over time, become a skilled practitioner (Manem 2010: 31). The knowledge of creating salt clearly fits these criteria: there were learnt traditions of knowledge involved, perhaps spreading back over centuries; there were physical acts and actions on matter; there was a mental idea of the end product and the processes which had to be gone through in order to create the desired product. And that technical knowledge ("know-how", as continental colleagues are fond of calling it) is intimately related to social aspects. As Lemonnier remarked,

> *"On the one hand, the human actors, sources of energy, tools, raw materials, gestures and mental procedures involved in a given action aimed at obtaining some material result generally fit together physically... otherwise no tangible result would derive from their systemic interaction. On the other hand, beside their material function, in most instances some of these elements.... also cohere and play a role in some symbolic aspect of human life. For members of a culture or a society have "ideas" (which we will call "representations", whether they are conscious or not) about every element of a technical process: raw materials, sources of energy, tools, actors, where and when things should take place, etc. And these technical representations are part of wider symbolic systems"* (Lemonnier 1993: 4).

It is important, too, to realise that not all technical processes may appear to us modern observers as "logical", in other words using the most ergonomic method or cost-effective use of resources. While our assumption may be that people generally did things in the most efficient way they could, we can always point to instances where the opposite was true: otherwise, how could the builders of Stonehenge have constructed their monument using many stones from the west of Wales, around 235 km (almost 150 miles) distant, or the metalsmiths of Bronze Age Sardinia used copper ores from Cyprus when their own island was well endowed with the mineral?

Within any technological process there can be many variations: as Gosselain (1992: 584) remarked, "a technological process can involve many *chaînes opératoires*", so for each production technique one might identify a series of actions, involving motor skills and mental concepts of the desired end, that could be called operational chains. Roux too, and others, have discussed the way that each stage of the process of making pots is subject to a whole range of choices on the part of the potter (Roux 2010: 5).

In the case of salt production and the chain of technical processes involved, one must make a distinction between for instance the briquetage technique and the trough technique, since these are completely distinct and different processes, neither of which was adopted in the region of the other (or so it seems).

	PRODUCTION PROCESS								
	Production of the raw material						Manufacture of salt		
NATURE AND ORDER OF OPERATIONS	Cut and spread out the canes	Cut and haul firewood for the pyre and oven	Construct the pyre	Gather and stack the dry canes	Monitor burning of the pyre	Build a shelter for the ashes	Fill bamboo containers with filtered water and transport to workshop	Monitor evaporation	Wrap the bars of salt
PRODUCT TRANSFORMATION	*Coix gigantea J. Kœnig*				Ashes		Brine	Rock salt	
PERSONS EMPLOYED	Group of women (2 women)	Individual men		Group of men and women (10 persons)	Individual men		Individual men		Group of men
DURATION OF EACH TASK	2 days	2 days	½ day	½ day	1 night	1 day	2 days	5 days and nights	1½ hours per bar
TOTAL DAYS WORKED	2 x 2 = 4 days	2 days	½ day	½ x 10 = 5 days	½ day	1 day	2 days	3 days	22 h = 3 days
	TOTAL DAYS OF WORK TO PRODUCE 15 BARS OF SALT = 21 DAYS						TOTAL DAYS OF WORK PER BAR = 1¼ DAYS		

Fig. 9.1. Process of salt production among the Baruya of New Guinea, according to M. Godelier (1969)

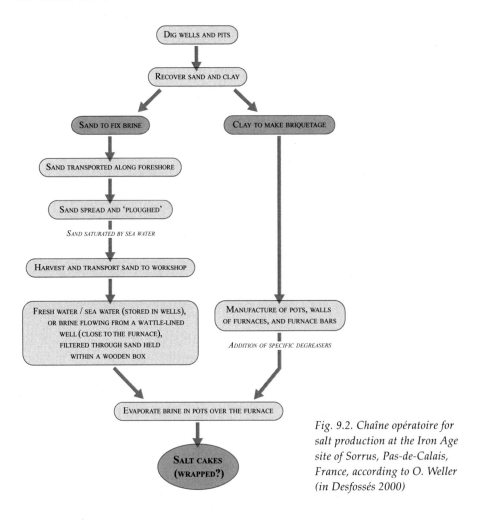

Fig. 9.2. Chaîne opératoire for salt production at the Iron Age site of Sorrus, Pas-de-Calais, France, according to O. Weller (in Desfossés 2000)

Several authors have written about the potential *chaînes opératoires* for salt-making using brine or salty sand. Godelier (1969) provided one for the "production process" of salt-making by the Baruya (Fig. 9.1). Archaeological examples include Prilaux (2000: 66 ff.), Weller (in Desfossés 2000: 344 Fig. 81) (Fig. 9.2), Daire (2003: 28), Olivier (2010: 154-5) and others. A recent attempt is that by Terán Manrique and Morgado (2011: 240 ff.).

The chain for briquetage must be similar to that for coarse pottery, except that the scope for variation was limited by the technological objectives to be achieved (the boiling of brine). Thus in general the aim was to make flat pans or parallelepiped containers, supported by pedestals, and small chalice-like cups in which the crystals could be accumulated. There was no need for the clay to be more than roughly sorted, and only enough filler needed to be added to ensure that the vessels did not crack when heat was applied to them; lumps of clay were simply moulded by hand into the required shapes; no surface elaboration or decoration was required. This is not to say that no choices were present at all, but they were distinctly limited.

On the other hand, taking the whole process of production from start to finish, saltmakers had distinct chains of production to follow. In tabular form these are:

Identify brine springs (or locations for boiling sea water)
Locate timber supplies/make charcoal
Collect brine in suitable containers
Construct a fireplace
Make a griddle/support for the vessels / Make pedestals
Make trays
Introduce brine
Continue to maintain the fire/ introduce air/ work bellows
Monitor the boiling process / regulate the heat to prevent cracking of the vessels
Collect crystals and place in chalices or other vessels, add fresh water
Reboil and repeat as necessary (till the salt is pure enough for human consumption)
Allow to cool
Pack crystals into carrying containers (organic or ceramic)
Repeat
Distribute the product
Abandon the site and create another

For the trough technique the chain was quite different. (I am assuming here that the technique involved is the first offered above, that of allowing water to drip onto rock salt.)

Identify brine springs and/or rock salt outcrops
Locate timber supplies
Fashion troughs, poles, wattle fences etc
Set up the assembly
Clear the rock face

Introduce fresh water into channels, running into the troughs

Monitor the dripping water and resultant depressions over several hours

Introduce wedges into the cracks and depressions thus formed

Break off chunks of rock

Grind the chunks to a powder / Place the rock in storage tanks to increase the salinity of the stored brine

Collect crystals

Pack crystals into containers (organic or ceramic)

Repeat

Distribute the product

Obvious though these processes may seem when written in black and white, for the people on the ground who did the work each involved a series of learnt actions, tried out and repeated until practiced perfectly. Most of them involve the expenditure of considerable effort; all of them require know-how. That know-how was intimately connected with a series of other pieces of knowledge, acquired through life from a range of crafts and skills. In this, we can suppose that one craft fed off and fed into another: there was interaction between the different crafts.

Nor were these chains or processes restricted to the actual production: they must apply also to distribution. This means not just the loading of animals or boats, the planning and execution of journeys so that convenient and safe stopping points might be met with, and all the attendant logistics; but also the social mechanisms involved in the actual exchange of salt. We have no means of knowing quite how this worked; ethnography might be our best source of ideas. In North Africa, the camel caravans travelled across the desert to great entrepôts on rivers or the sea, whence the salt cakes entered a more formal trade network. By contrast, in 16th century Columbia, salt was passed down the line from hand to hand, getting more and more expensive and difficult to obtain as it went, "until it was used only by the chiefs, the common people making do with salt processed from palms and human urine" (Cardale-Schrimpff 1975).

Cross-craft interaction

Cross-craft interaction is the process by which skills learnt in, and applied to, one craft are applied to a different one (Brysbaert 2011; McGovern & Notis 1989). Studies in the Aegean have covered a variety of craft skills relating to pottery, painted plaster, and stone and metalwork.

In the context of ancient salt, there are obvious interactions with potting (in the case of briquetage) and with woodworking (with the trough technique). The interaction with potting is perhaps not very significant, given the coarseness and crudity of briquetage, though it is noteworthy that in some cases what appear to be "ordinary" pots were used for the boiling of brine (thus there is no real briquetage in the Criş culture sites of Moldavia, or at Chalcolithic Provadia: in both cases the excavators have assumed that standard pots were used for the purpose). The interaction with woodworking, on the other hand, was very significant. In a Bronze Age context, the troughs used in the Carpathian zone have obvious similarities

Fig. 9.3. The joints in the timber-lined shafts of Iron Age date at Băile Figa, Beclean, Romania (photo: Author)

to log canoes and to coffins, though they appear to be more crudely fashioned (and had no need for operational stability as canoes did). Some of the remarkable constructional elements recovered in excavation in Romania show facets and joints on structural timbers, which must have been acquired in centuries of carpentry for house-building and the like. As well as roundwood used as poles, substantial timbers were adzed to create planks and boards, and a range of pieces were used as wedges or sprung devices to ensure constructional elements stayed firmly in place. Ladders – substantial items, with broad flat rungs – are also present. It is impossible to know how many of these were invented for the purpose; it is more likely that such techniques existed independent of salt-making, and were adapted for the purpose.

In the Iron Age a completely different set of structures were made. These consisted of wood-lined shafts, with a very specific type of joint between uprights and horizontal members (Fig. 9.3). In these, the end of the timber was either cut at right-angles across three-quarters of its width, leaving a projecting tongue or spur which lapped against the upright; or the cut was rounded, the surface resting snugly against the upright. At the other end, the pole was tapered and scarfed to fit against the side of the upright, which was chamfered to take it. These joints are not sophisticated, but they seem to have been effective, and were presumably used regularly in timber work for other constructions.

The other remarkable Iron Age construction recovered in the excavations in Romania was a ladder, over 5 m long with a number of preserved rungs (Fig. 6.5). To quote the specialist who studied it:

The sides were boxed trunks, neatly chamfered at the edges, with a gently curving side profiles. There were at least seven rungs on the most complete side, which penetrated rectangular holes in the side timbers. The rungs were very carefully fashioned, with a gracefully carved taper towards the middle and well finished tenons which were pegged in place on the outer side of the mortise holes through a square hole at either end (Brunning in Harding & Kavruk 2010; 2013).

One may presume that the technique used for this piece was well-known in carpentry at the time; ladders must have been normal pieces of equipment in the Iron Age, as in earlier and later periods.

Perhaps more significant is the potential for interaction with mining for other materials, notably for copper and gold. In each case, the commodity desired was largely hidden underground and had to be revealed by means of a greater or lesser degree of earth-moving, and of forceful removal of the hard mineral from its parent rock. In some parts of Europe, metals and salt appear close together in the earth, as is the case with the eastern Alps or Transylvania. In such a situation, skills from one might have been utilised in the other; this might have applied most obviously to Hallstatt or the Dürrnberg, where salt was mined from deep shafts. Of course deep mining technology goes back to the Neolithic, with the extraction of flint from mines in various parts of Europe. Much is known about Roman mining from textual sources (notably Pliny the Elder, *Natural History*, Books 33-34), as well as from archaeological finds (e.g. Wollmann 1996), but these are not our concern here.[31]

The superficial extraction of rock salt, as seen in Romania, has more in common with quarrying for stone, such as occurred in the Neolithic for the production of stone axes. Fire-setting was often used in ancient mining, but this was not the technique used in this case, as far as one can tell. The use of water to create cracks and depressions by dripping onto the salt surface has no known parallels in other crafts. In this case it would appear that the technology was the result of innovation, perhaps after many centuries of observation and experimentation.

In summary, while salt production was in many ways *sui generis*, there was plenty of scope for techniques usually found in other crafts to be utilised in the various forms of salt manufacture. Potting and carpentry were the most obvious; mining technology is more ambiguous, and certain technical aspects are peculiar to salt. As for interaction in the opposite direction, there are no clear indications. But given that salt was a crucial commodity, everyone in society must have known about it and many must have witnessed its procurement; so there was ample scope for cross-fertilization of technologies to occur.

---

31 The Bible often mentions metals but only once refers to their extraction: 'Surely there is a vein for the silver, and a place for gold where they fine it. Iron is taken out of the earth, and brass [sc. copper or bronze] is molten out of the stone' (Job 28:1-2).

Commoditization/Commodification

Salt as it exists in the earth is a raw material like any other, and in itself of little use. To be useful, it needs to be worked in some manner. Once extracted and ground, or evaporated, it becomes an economically useful material which may be exchanged, in other words a commodity. This process of commoditization (in anthropology also sometimes called commodification) is something that has been studied by many authors (notably Appadurai 1986; Kopytoff 1986). Commodities are things that have value, specifically exchange value; that value is not inherent but assigned by the people involved in an exchange – just as an Old Master painting has no significant value inherent in the canvas or the paint, but in what people are prepared to pay for it as a painting.

In an archaeological context, metals have been discussed by several authors in the context of commoditization (Primas 1997; Renfrew 1986; Shennan 1993). Since copper and gold were materials that were new to the world in the Neolithic, they clearly developed from being unusual substances, to more common things, and eventually to materials which could be exchanged as items of value. Primas has discussed this in the context of increasing quantities of bronze in the Early Bronze Age (Primas 1997), and Shennan in that of the production of copper in the Austrian Alps (Shennan 1993). Shennan considered the process by which copper acquired value as an exchangeable substance and salt is no different in this respect – though the process of commoditization occurred earlier than with copper. How and when this took place is a matter for speculation, but one can argue that once exploitation was regularised, and in particular once the scale of production increased from a low-level, apparently haphazard, enterprise to something involving considerable numbers of people and a substantial quantity of produced salt, then it had acquired value and become a commodity. This seems to be the case in those instances where one can suggest an industrial scale of production, as I have for Transylvania in the Bronze Age, and for several parts of France in the Iron Age; probably for any area where the movement of salt in exchange can be demonstrated. Salt that was exchanged in this way had already become a commodity; the transition from raw material needed for domestic use to trade good seems to have occurred in the second half of the second millennium BC and became consolidated in the first.

Technological innovation

Why people adopt one technology rather than another is a matter many authors, especially in France, have debated. And once one technology was in place, what caused it to change, or not to change? How did innovation in technological processes occur? Why, on the other hand, did it not occur when a demonstrably more efficient process was available? Among the answers that can be offered to the last question are: innate conservatism (preferring the known to the unknown, identifying oneself by a particular set of cultural and technological values, assuming one's technical methods are superior without any experimentation to validate the belief), lack of knowledge of alternatives, lack of resources to implement the change, and social effects. The latter have commonly been seen as particularly important, in that technologies are embedded in economy and society; there is a reciprocal interplay of influence to and fro between them.

When we look at the technology of salt production, the first question is: why did the different salt "zones" (i.e. technologies) exist? Why did some groups adopt briquetage and stick with it, even though other methods were possible? More pertinent perhaps, why did people use the trough technique when in much of the rest of Europe people were using briquetage, and briquetage had been used in the same area in the Neolithic? If it is correct to assume that the trough technique was only applicable to areas with rock salt on the earth's surface, then it is probably understandable that it was not used at the main production sites in Germany or France. The reverse is not true, however: given the abundance of brine springs in the Trough Zone, briquetage could have worked just as well there as in western Europe.

The adoption of new technologies comes about in a number of ways. Mostly crudely, one can distinguish between the "flash of genius" process, where one person just thinks up a new way of doing something (as it might be the invention of the wheel or the discovery of penicillin) and the "follow my neighbour" process, where ideas are transmitted culturally (i.e. socially) across geographical space. In the last, new technologies arrive from outside and are adopted if they bring perceived advantages (or not to do so would bring disadvantages). But in the case of the first process, things are not usually so simple. Most discoveries and inventions depend on many previous efforts by a number of people or groups. As Brian Arthur points out (2009), technologies are combinations of other, smaller, technical processes. Novel elements in a technology are only made possible by existing technologies, or by combinations of such technologies, and occur within a social framework and are "shaped by social needs" (Arthur 2009: 108). Arthur distinguishes what he calls the "basic concept", which must then be embodied in physical form, using the "sub-assemblies" or functional groupings of technical processes of which they are formed.

Seen in this light, one can see how the briquetage technique changed dramatically over the centuries. In the Neolithic and Bronze Age, it appears that what was involved was a rather simple process of putting crude clay beakers or trays filled with brine into or over a fire, and boiling the brine until crystals could be picked off. No doubt there were many problems to overcome even with a process this simple (the propensity of the vessels to break when heat is applied to them, for instance), but compared to what followed in the Iron Age these problems seem minor. Once we arrive at the great installations seen in the Seille valley in the Iron Age, we have moved onto a different plane: the technology involves not just the containers but the construction of the furnace, griddle, and so on; each element had to be solved before production could achieve the quasi-industrial level assumed.

One can similarly imagine that the trough technique went through a series of sub-processes and iterations before it was perfected (if it ever was). The one element about which there is specific evidence is the change from round to square pegs in the trough base over the course of some 800 years; this can be explained by the fact that round pegs would turn in a round hole and potentially not be watertight; square pegs could not turn and might thus remain tightly in position.

Functional explanations of this kind may go some way to elucidating how and why technologies arose and changed, but since they are always socially situated, it is necessary too to consider how society might have affected them.

Salt and society

A number of authors have attempted a social reconstruction of salt-producing societies (Abarquero Moras *et al.* 2012: 321 ff.; Daire 2003: 137; Prilaux 2000: 104); a range of issues relating to the social and economic aspects of salt production have been considered by those outside Europe, for instance Rowan Flad for China (2011), or Heather McKillop for the Maya (2002). In this, much centres around quite how one imagines the relationship between producer and consumer. Were they two different sets of people, or one and the same? If the former, how did miners or salt-boilers pass on their product to other people outside their own domestic circle? If the latter, are we to assume that each person or family worked primarily in order to produce salt for the home, with the excess being made available for exchange outside the community? These are tricky questions to answer given the nature of the evidence.

French authors have been particularly assiduous in examining the nature of production, especially in the Iron Age, notably whether it was "domestic", "artisanal", or "industrial" (e.g. Daire 1994: 100 ff.; 2003: 122 ff.), in other words whether it was essentially a household activity producing salt for home consumption, the work of individual craftspeople to supply their own needs and exchange the surplus, or something more organised and on a much bigger scale; and whether it was something each producer could vary at will, or a technology introduced from outside. Most authorities agree that coastal production must have been seasonal. At the same time, it is evident that in France at least, the level of specialisation greatly increased over the course of the Iron Age, and by the Gallo-Roman period small sites where the technology varied from place to place had been conjoined into large areas where the same technique was used. One can debate how many furnaces, producing how much salt, might qualify for the term "industrial". Since there is good evidence for the large scale of this production, and the movement of the salt far inland (in England as well as France), it does not seem excessive to dub this production "industrial", even if we do not know who controlled or profited from it.

Prilaux also sees an increasing complexity of production through the course of the Iron Age, initially with very small production areas without any enclosure; giving way to a much more circumscribed pattern with the workshops strictly separated from their settlements by ditches and palisades (Prilaux 2000: 88 ff.). At the same time, the creation of the large griddle furnaces enabled a much greater quantity of salt to be produced at one time – with a single furnace able to produce hundreds of kilos of salt, and many furnaces operating simultaneously;

this compares with individual small furnaces producing a few tens of kilos in the earlier period (Daire 2003: 126 ff.).

Salt has been considered a factor of great importance not only for individuals but also for the wider society in which they lived, since control and possession of it promoted differences in the ability to control other commodities. Typically it has been assumed that salt enabled those who controlled its supply and distribution to accumulate wealth, as shown by grave-goods or deposited materials. Two cases stand out: the Early Iron Age mines of Hallstatt (and to a lesser extent the Dürrnberg); and the deposition of bronze in hoards in Transylvania, as discussed in Chapter 8. The Hallstatt case is more difficult to assess because traditionally it was supposed that those buried in the cemetery were not those who worked the mine, but it is now considered likely that they were in fact members of the mining workforce (see below).

Can salt be compared with metals in terms of its ability to articulate society, as gold is believed to have done? This might depend on a number of factors. First, how was the extraction of salt managed and controlled? Did local communities lay claim to their salt resources, monopolise them, preventing access to others? Or was there a free-for-all? Second, once extracted, how was the distribution of salt managed? The hypothesis that control of salt led to wealth in other commodities assumes that there was a significant level of community organisation at more than the village level, which could have enabled a community to manage the supply in such a way that valuables were supplied in return.

Some authors have discussed these matters in the context of specialization in production, seeing the organization of the production process as crucial to an understanding of the place of salt in society. Flad, for instance, has argued for concentration of production on the basis of the forms and quantities of briquetage-like ceramic present on his Zhongba site; a rigidly defined organization of space was created over time, though the features recovered suggest that production was a seasonal affair, at least in the latest phase (Flad 2011: 172). For Abarquero Moras and colleagues (2012), the mysterious and magical qualities of salt are seen as important, enabling elites to manipulate society through the practising of a range of ritual activities (signs of which they claim to have found at Santioste and Molino Sanchón II, in the form of pits containing animal bones, cereal macrofossils, pottery and stones), including feasting and various kinds of intentional deposition. This is in addition to the ways in which salt may have been controlled by elite groups in the Beaker period and Early Bronze Age, evidence of which comes, it is suggested, from well-provisioned graves in and around the salt production areas.

De León has considered the question of whether Aztec salt production was a domestic activity in the area near Lake Texcoco, and if it was, whether it was a full-time or part-time business (De León 2009). Here, production seems to have taken place in the dry season, in other words it was a seasonal activity, and household-based rather than industrial in nature: a "skilled domestic craft that produced for export and was practised *intermittently* (i.e. seasonally) alongside a variety of other subsistence activities" (ibid. 53). The household nature of this production fits well with what we understand about much of prehistoric European salt production, at least until the Iron Age.

Some dictators in the 20th century were very successful in manipulating the economy so that even in very poor countries they maintained a grotesquely high standard of living, while their subjects eked out a miserable existence on or below the breadline. People have become rich in most societies throughout history. In this, the ability of the community to procure resources is important; but how those resources are then channelled is the crucial aspect. Clearly many ancient societies, certainly from the start of the Bronze Age onwards if not before, had a hierarchical structure, with wealth and status unequally distributed. While the Varna cemetery seems to be an early example of this phenomenon, it is unique for its period; it is otherwise only with the advent of metals that social articulation on a large scale became possible. I pass over here developments in Mesopotamia or Egypt from the later fourth millennium BC onwards, though these are also relevant to the discussion. During the course of the Bronze Age in Europe, such differentiation became more and more marked; and by the Early Iron Age, with extraordinarily rich burials like that from Hochdorf, the process was complete.

The Hochdorf and comparable burials, dating to the late sixth century BC, are contemporary with the Iron Age exploitation of the Hallstatt mine, but their local context does not suggest any particular linkage with salt. The phenomenon of increasing display in grave-goods in the Early Iron Age was arguably something connected with other phenomena than salt: the opening up of trade routes to the Mediterranean, for instance, and the emulation by local potentates of developing power structures south of the Alps. In this, trade in salt was only one of a number of commercial developments that affected communities in central Europe as well as in Italy and elsewhere.

To what extent could we imagine that the massive Iron Age production of salt in the Seille valley, or the potentially equally large production in Transylvania in both Bronze and Iron Ages, produced a comparable effect on society? For the Transylvanian situation it is certainly not possible to see any such effect in terms of burial wealth; it is the deposited bronze that would come into question. For Lorraine the situation is equally uncertain. Modelling economy and society in these areas would need to take into account a range of factors. The area of northern Transylvania where the largest amount of evidence survives is not rich in either hoards or burials, though metals must have circulated here, as elsewhere. The scale of production has been argued to have been considerable and intended for distribution beyond the home area; yet there are no signs that this brought about any significant uplift in general "wealth" in the region.

The appearance of briquetage in graves, discussed by Jockenhövel (2012) (above), is perhaps significant in this respect, not because it indicates wealth or status as such, but because of the symbolic link it suggests with salt production, distribution and consumption. In this sense, salt may have had more of a symbolic value – much as ancient authors discussed it in terms of its effect on the human character – than a "monetary" one (i.e. as it was valued in exchange terms).

The case for a marked social effect brought about by salt thus remains unproven. Even at Hallstatt, one can argue that the richness of many graves is a reflection of wider processes at work, seen at many other places at the same time, and not specifically related to salt. In France, it has been noted that cemeteries close to and of the same period as salt production sites do not contain especially rich graves (Prilaux 2000: 104-5).

Gender aspects

Who carried out the work on salt production sites? How heavy was the work? What ancillary aspects need to be considered? To what extent can we imagine that women were involved as well as men?

Pany and Teschler-Nicola (2007) have shown that women at Iron Age Hallstatt had indications of strong marks in the muscles involved in flexing the elbow and supporting, lifting or pulling heaving loads, in some cases exceeding those on male skeletons. These marks suggest a role in hammering (probably by picks to detach blocks of salt, using the "hearts" that are known from the mines: Kern *et al.* 2009: 88), and in carrying (presumably loads of rock from the working face to the processing areas). Women at Hallstatt seem to have done the same hard work as men, and had just as hard a life, on the basis of this data – at least in the Early Iron Age. In the absence of a Bronze Age cemetery of this date at this location it is speculative to assume that the same applied at that period, but there is no reason not to do so.

There has long been speculation about the identity of those buried in the Iron Age cemetery at Hallstatt: were they the miners, or rather those who simply controlled the mines and acquired wealth and prestige on the proceeds? Given the results of the anthropological analysis, it would appear that it is the former which was the case – which might appear somewhat strange in today's world. In reality, we should not be surprised that a community of salt-miners lived and died close to their place of work, and was buried with the artefacts which trade and exchange had brought them – even if the finding of weaponry in the form of swords and daggers is more surprising.

Laurent Olivier (2010: 155) points to the finds of schist and lignite rings in the debris at Marsal "la Digue", which other sites in the region show to have been part of female dress attire. Such women who were present at Marsal might, in his opinion, be considered "associated with the processes of salt production, in the interior of the workshop"; this might have included the work of concentrating and storing the brine, and of carrying the concentrated liquid in wooden containers, one of which was found on the site.

Gender in salt production has also been considered briefly by Elaine Morris (Morris 2007: 440-1) and Janice Kinory (2012: 25; 125-6). Kinory made use of analogies with pottery production, as discussed by Arnold (1985) and Peacock (1981). Here it is primarily the production of the briquetage that is under consideration, since studies of pottery production in ethnographic situations show that pot-making is often women's preserve, especially if a range of fabrics and forms were being made. Coarse pottery such as briquetage, formed by hand and fired at relatively low temperatures (even perhaps in a simple bonfire), could have been the preserve of either sex, and the relatively undemanding nature of such production in terms of physical strength certainly makes it possible that both sexes were involved. Morris suggests that in the Lincolnshire Fenlands in the first millennium BC it would only be with the intensification of production in the later Iron Age that a more complex structure involving both men and women might have developed, and that the simple production of the first phase could have been the responsibility of women. But there is no real evidence to confirm this other than (potentially) the finger- and thumb-prints on the crudely made pedestals, which could indicate different hand sizes and therefore either or both sexes.

In this discussion one may distinguish between the making of the briquetage containers, and the production of the salt itself; and assumptions about gender roles will here depend on the technique of production. Even if women at Hallstatt took part in heavy tasks one might expect that those tasks requiring the toughest work would have required male strength.

In other types of salt production, one may speculate on the role of women in the various kinds of work. The Hallstatt evidence strongly suggests that physical strength was not the sole criterion for those taking part in the mining activities; so there would be no reason in principle why women as well as men could not have been involved in all the tasks that the "trough technique" involved in the Carpathian Basin. Of these the hardest would appear to be the use of picks or sledge-hammers to crack and break up the rock, but collecting up and carrying the broken pieces for processing, putting them in storage pools for evaporation and concentration, collecting salt crystals, making salt cakes – all these would be perfectly possible even for those without great physical strength. This is to say nothing of the tasks involving the manufacture of the wooden structures: the felling of trees (some sizeable), transporting the timber to the site, doing the carpentry to create the various structures involved, erecting and commissioning them, and running them once in operation. In the Iron Age this involved climbing down into shafts or pits and hacking at the rock face; in the Bronze Age there is less evidence for such deep shafts, but instead the use of the troughs, storage tanks or pools, and other constructions of uncertain use.

Removing blocks of rock salt from an outcrop is usually extremely hard work. Even with a bulldozer, experimental observations in Romania found that the rock surface would only be scored by the teeth of the bucket rather than broken up into lumps (Buzea 2010). Observations of a peasant in the village of Dumitra near Bistriţa, working with a 15 kg cast iron axe, showed that it took him some fifteen minutes to detach a piece of salt of modest size (Deák 2008).[32] These are salutary facts when considering the extent to which women might have been involved in work at the rock face, especially with Bronze Age tools.

---

32   As shown on the video recording made in April 2007 when the team visited Dumitra.

The Hallstatt case depended on the existence of the large Iron Age cemetery, where the bones of the deceased could be the subject of detailed anthropological analysis. That is instructive but unusual, even in an Iron Age context. In a Bronze Age context such a linkage is not currently known to exist, though presumably the bodies of some Bronze Age miners are preserved somewhere. Here the experience of recent work in Iran may be helpful, where bodies are preserved in a salt mine (Aali *et al.* 2012a; Aali *et al.* 2012b; Schachner 2004).

Ethnographic situations can provide analogies for labour division in salt production, but this is not necessarily helpful for archaeological situations. First, there are examples where men did the work and others where it was regarded as women's work; second, though some of the technologies are similar to what we can reconstruct for European prehistory, others are quite different. For instance, Godelier (1969: 12) found among the Baruya that the initial tasks of gathering the salt plants and burning them, and constructing shelter for the ashes, were equally divided between men and women, but the specialist task of constructing the furnace, placing the moulds in place, and evaporating the brine, was strictly a male preserve. In parts of Mexico, saltmaking is considered women's activity, with the knowledge being passed down from mother to daughter or granddaughter (Good 1995). By contrast, in Guatemala salt-making used to be considered a male enterprise (Reina & Monaghan 1981). These examples simply show that there is no one way of dividing salt making between the sexes in modern times; the same is no doubt true for the ancient world. It varied from place to place and period to period.

Provisioning production sites

Another aspect which has been the subject of recent debate is the matter of supplies to the mining areas (Kowarik 2009; Kowarik & Reschreiter 2010). Given that the conditions for arable agriculture in the Alpine area are markedly less favourable than in the pre-Alpine lake area, any climatic change might well have caused problems, forcing the inhabitants of such areas to seek supplies from further afield. Especially after the 9th century cal BC, such changes might have caused a crisis in food supplies and an increase in mobility between Alpine and pre-Alpine areas. This could even have led to smaller mining communities, better adapted to the smaller carrying capacity of the area (Kowarik & Reschreiter 2011). At the same time, supra-regional contacts could have facilitated an increase in salt production.

The end of the Bronze Age phase of exploitation at Hallstatt might be connected with the maximum of the Löbben oscillation, and a significant worsening of the climate which might have led to increased mobility.

There are significant differences in Bronze and Iron Age methods of working at Hallstatt. Virtually all the materials needed for salt extraction were available at or near the site itself; these included the various woods (oak, lime bast etc), which in the succeeding period were absent or almost so. Similarly, a range of specialized equipment was in use in the Bronze Age, whereas in the Iron Age only the pick was (apparently) used; one may speculate whether this was a technological choice or one forced on the miners by environmental conditions (such as climatic). According to the observations made by Kowarik and Reschreiter, more than a tenth of the broken salt lumps was left unused in the mine in the Iron Age, in direct contrast to the Bronze Age situation, where every piece of broken salt rock was used (Kowarik & Reschreiter 2011: 251-2).

The production process by the trough technique has equally significant implications for provisioning: the acquisition and supply of wood was a major concern, even if shaping it into the complex forms required meant that wood-workers were also crucially important. It is not known at present how large a quantity of wood was involved at the various sites in the north of Transylvania; it would appear that the local environment was capable of supplying these needs without great difficulty, certainly by comparison with the timber needs of the enormous fortified sites that arose in the Late Bronze Age, in the Banat and elsewhere (Szentmiklosi *et al.* 2011).

Clay for making briquetage was unlikely to be in short supply, as much of this ceramic was crude and coarse, though there were specific recipes that had to be followed. The provision of wood for the furnaces might have been a different matter, however: one possibility is that the Red Hills of eastern England came to an end because the time and labour required to transport the timber to the firing sites became uneconomic.

Since it is not known in many cases in what form salt was transported, it is not possible to make sensible predictions about the provisioning needs as far as containers were concerned, or indeed the requirements in terms of transport technology; but since heavier materials in the form of metal ores and raw metal was demonstrably transported over long distances, the movement of salt would not appear to present special difficulties in this respect.

Towards a new narrative of salt production

The various aspects discussed above provide opportunities for a new approach, or series of approaches, to the understanding of salt in ancient societies, especially prehistoric ones. The first issue is the role of salt. Most authorities have stressed that salt is a physiological need for humans and animals, as well as being important as an anti-bacterial agent, used for preserving foodstuffs and assisting the healing of wounds. Fewer have dwelt on the symbolic aspect, in which salt served a role as a medium of social interaction. Flad has suggested that salt was a luxury, serving social rather than physiological needs (Flad 2011: 33); while it is true that the need for salt has been exaggerated by some authorities it is still the case that most societies seek out salt to add to food, primarily for reasons of taste though one supposes that this is linked to the physiological need for an intake of salt for the chemical balance of the body.

The question then arises, were the lengths to which ancient societies went to get salt linked entirely, or even mainly, to these bodily needs (taste and chemical balance)? Given that these lengths were very great, even extreme, one has to question this assumption. If most prehistoric societies for which we have evidence of salt production were actually meat and fish eaters, then most of their physiological needs for salt would have been catered for by their diet. Taste is another matter; most modern people think that food, notably meat, tastes better when salt is added during the cooking, but equally one can condition oneself to little or no salt. And for many prehistoric communities it is far from clear how they got access to supplies of salt. Many, indeed, may not have sought additional salt, or only small quantities of it, and not suffered undue consequences.

At the same time, it seems far-fetched to imagine that salt was entirely a symbolic or even a ritual matter. Certainly it is possible to show in historical and ethnographic situations that salt serves a role in tradition and ritual, for instance in the *mola salsa* or salted meal of the Romans, without which no sacrifice could be carried out,[33] but this does not involve large amounts and is more symbolic than commercial. It is argued above that only rather pure salt would be suitable for this purpose, and this would involve the use of particular sources, or a particular set of processes to remove impurities. The production of salt in industrial quantities cannot be seen in this light; it must have been intended for distribution among communities both local and regional – even supraregional.

The hope that physical analysis will soon solve the major problems relating to distribution among Bronze and Iron Age communities raises the prospect of answering some of these questions. At the same time, the progress of work in palaeobiology means that questions relating to gender roles are also resolvable. If this happens, we will indeed have a new narrative of ancient salt to relate.

---

33 maxime tamen in sacris intellegitur auctoritas, quando nulla conficiuntur sine mola salsa (Pliny, *Natural History* XXXI, 89).

Chapter 10

Conclusions and prospects

In this book I have surveyed the situation regarding salt in European prehistory, concentrating on those technologies and areas which offer the fullest information on how and when salt was produced and distributed. Much is now known that was unclear or totally unknown until recently; much remains to be elucidated by future scholars.

Among the main achievements of salt archaeology in the last 20 years are these:

- A full understanding of briquetage forms
- A clear picture of the processes of salt boiling in many regions
- A fuller understanding of the use of wooden troughs and attendant installations
- A good understanding of the locations of coastal production in the Graeco-Roman world, and presumptively of the preceding centuries

The things that we do not know about ancient salt and which we need to know include:

- An understanding of how salt was obtained in saltless areas
- An understanding of the ways in which salt was moved from salt-rich to salt-poor areas
- The ability to identify salt from specific sources
- The ability to identify ancient salt residues on pottery
- A better knowledge of the identity of those who carried out the production work – age, gender, status
- An understanding of the scale and nature of production, e.g. whether "artisanal" or "industrial"

The progress of research is already addressing several of these unknowns, as discussed above, and future work will no doubt tackle most of the others.

Salt today

World Heritage and related sites

Three sites or areas in Europe concerned specifically with salt production are inscribed on the UNESCO World Heritage list: Salins-les-Bains / Arc-et-Senans ("From the Great Saltworks of Salins-les-Bains to the Royal Saltworks of Arc-et-Senans, the Production of Open-pan Salt") near Besançon (Grassias 2008; Scachetti 2008) (Fig. 10.1); Hallstatt ("the Hallstatt-Dachstein / Salzkammergut Cultural

Fig. 10.1. The UNESCO World Heritage site of Arc-les-Senans / Salins les Bains (photo: Mihai-bogdan Lazar, Dreamstime.com)

Fig. 10.2. The UNESCO World Heritage site of Wieliczka (photo: Jorge Duarte Estevao, Dreamstime.com).

Fig. 10.3. Part of the salt production attraction at Solivar, Prešov, Slovakia (photo: Author)

Landscape") (Fig. 6.3); and Wieliczka and Bochnia ("Wieliczka and Bochnia Royal Salt Mines") in southern Poland (Fig. 10.2). The latter two have been discussed several times in this account, while the first, as a production facility of recent centuries, is not directly relevant to prehistory.

Wieliczka was visited by over 1.1 million visitors in 2012 (http://www. wieliczka-saltmine.com/news/archive/visiting), much the largest number visiting any of the sites mentioned – no doubt partly because of its proximity to Kraków and Oświęcim (Auschwitz). Hallstatt is also a very popular tourist destination, lying as it does in beautiful Alpine scenery; between May and October 2012 more than 104,000 visitors entered the mine.[34] Each of these sites offers a different visitor experience, given their different technological histories.

Several other European salt mines are visitable, for instance Turda, Cacica and Praid in Romania, Berchtesgaden in Bavaria, Cardona in Catalonia, or Kłodawa in Poland. The experience of going deep into the ground in search of salt is impressive, but for the most part divorced from prehistoric reality. Where, as at Hallstatt, miners did work underground, they did not carve out huge straight-sided caverns hundreds of feet in length and dozens high, like modern salt mines, but cramped and narrow shafts and tunnels. At the same time, there are similarities: prehistoric equivalents to the shrines to St Barbara (patron saint of miners), that are commonly found in salt mines of historical date, were no doubt present in some pre-Christian form.

---

34 Information kindly provided by Hans Reschreiter and Kerstin Kowarik.

As well as mines, there are museums and other production sites. Solivar, at Prešov in eastern Slovakia, is another impressive example of a historic saltworks that has become a tourist attraction (Fig. 10.3) – arguably just as worthy to join the UNESCO list as some of the sites mentioned above; salt is still produced in a modern factory in the town. Salt museums are present in a number of places, most notably Lüneburg in northern Germany, where the Deutsches Salzmuseum has a comprehensive display of modern and historical salt production, both in the area and elsewhere. The Weaver Hall Museum (formerly Salt Museum) in Northwich, Cheshire, UK, is modest in scale and deals mostly with local history. The Halloren and Salinemuseum in Halle/Saale (Sachsen-Anhalt) is concerned with salt production, mostly in historical times, in that area; while the Riserva naturale integrale Saline di Trapani e Paceco in western Sicily has a saltworks museum in the nature reserve.[35] Clearly salt production has been regarded by museum people and local authorities as having good tourist potential, though observations on site suggest that there is a significant task facing them to get the public to realise that salt is a commodity that is not only vital to life, but one that someone has to obtain from the world around, often at the cost of enormous effort, rather than simply involving a trip to the supermarket.

Salt and climate change

A number of authors have pointed out, notably as long ago as fifty years by M.R. Bloch (1963: 98) that much salt is produced on low-lying coastal strips, most only a few metres above sea-level, and production is thus at the mercy of rising sea levels. This is very much the case with production on Mediterranean shores, and perhaps even more on Atlantic coasts, notably in France. One may therefore question what the future holds for these production sites, given the continuing rise in atmospheric carbon, the consequent warming of the climate, and – inevitably – the ensuing melting of polar ice and concomitant sea level rise. It is known that global sea level has risen by some 20 cm since 1870, nearly half of that since 1950. Projections into the future depend on many variables, but most envisage a faster rise in the next 50 years than the last. Some scenarios see a rise of over 2 feet (61 cm) at coastal cities such as New York or London by 2100, with much higher water during storms, for instance on Atlantic and North Sea coasts. In such a situation, sea salt production in its present locations along western French shores will surely have to cease or move. The same must be true for other sea salt producers, which by definition lie on or near the sea.

This is not to say, of course, that such production will cease: the sea and its salt will always be there, and exploitable. Production will have to move inland with the sea as it encroaches on more land. But the effects will be very different in different countries. Those countries that get most of their salt from mines, like the UK or Poland, will not see much change. Those that get it from the sea, like France and Mediterranean countries, will have to adapt to a greater or lesser degree.

---

35   Information on these sites, all of which I have visited with the exception of the last, is available on their websites.

Salt globally is not, of course, in short supply, even if producers in specific locations are forced to close or adapt. The US, by far the largest producer in the world, has enormous underground reserves, and even a modest-sized country like the UK is self-sufficient in salt and likely to remain so for the foreseeable future. Mines do have to go deeper, and that brings attendant costs, not only those of bringing the salt to the surface but also those concerning the greater heat of the mining environment at greater depths, the need to consider underground threats to human safety, the need to pump out water from deeper down, and other considerations. Nevertheless, salt is abundant and cheap, and likely to remain so, even for countries that have to import much or all of it. As discussed above, the great majority of salt is used for industrial purposes or as road salt; while the need for the former will continue, the latter is hardly a necessity of life, and many countries do not salt their roads in winter as a matter of course, or only do so in towns. The small amount that is consumed in human food is never likely to run out.

The future of salt from the past

Understanding ancient salt is a concern for salt archaeologists, both from the technical point of view and as far as the economy of ancient societies is concerned. Those who work specifically on ancient salt have made a concerted effort in recent years to bring salt archaeology centre-stage in the understanding of ancient societies; with mixed results, however. Nevertheless, there are signs that more and more scholars accept the importance of salt within the ancient economy.

The general public, however, has little knowledge or understanding of salt archaeology. Presentations of the spectacular results of recent work are often received with surprise, even amazement, that such extraordinary installations can survive in such good condition. Here archaeology has a task to do, since many of the locations where archaeological salt survives are fragile or threatened – by development, by agriculture, or by environmental change. How to preserve such sites for the future is a major problem: at some there is little to see on the ground, at others there may be pressures from the needs of modern living to change site environments irrevocably.

It should be clear from the foregoing, however, that ancient salt in Europe was a major industry affecting the lives of all who lived with it. Fugitive though its traces may sometimes be, it is worth developing a strategy to preserve as much of what remains as is feasible, for the education and enjoyment of present and future generations.

Selected accounts in ancient authors

Pliny the Elder (Gaius Plinius Secundus, AD 23-79), *Natural History* Book XXXI, 73-92 (Bailey 1929; Healy 1999)

1. "All salt is artificial or native; each is formed in several ways, but there are two agencies, condensation or drying up of water. It is dried out of the Tarentine lake by summer sun, when the whole pool turns into salt, although it is always shallow, never exceeding knee height, likewise in Sicily from a lake, called Cocanicus, and from another near Gela. Of these the edges only dry up; in Phrygia, Cappadocia, and at Aspendus, the evaporation is wider, in fact right to the centre. There is yet another wonderful thing about it: the same amount is restored during the night as is taken away during the day. All salt from pools is fine powder, and not in blocks. Another kind produced from sea water spontaneously is foam left on the edge of the shore and on rocks. All this is condensation from drift, and that found on rocks has the sharper taste. There are also three different kinds of native salt; for in Bactria are two vast lakes, one facing the Scythians, the other the Arii, which exude salt, while at Citium in Cyprus and around Memphis salt is taken out of a lake and then dried in the sun. But the surface too of rivers may condense into salt, the rest of the stream flowing as it were under ice, as near the Caspian Gates are what are called "rivers of salt," also around the Mardi and the Armenians. Moreover, in Bactria too the rivers Ochus and Oxus bring down scrapings of salt from nearby mountains.

2. "There are also lakes in Africa, and that muddy ones, which carry salt. Indeed hot springs too carry it, such as those at Pagasae. So much for the different kinds of salt which come, as natural products, from waters.

3. "There are also mountains of natural salt, such as Oromenus in India, where it is cut out like blocks of stone from a quarry, and ever replaces itself, bringing greater revenues to the rajahs than those from gold and pearls. It is also dug out of the earth in Cappadocia, being evidently formed by condensation of moisture. Here indeed it is split into sheets like mica; the blocks are very heavy, nicknamed by the people "grains." At Gerra, a town of Arabia, the walls and houses are made of blocks of salt cemented with water. Near Pelusium too King Ptolemy found salt when he was making a camp. This led afterwards to the discovery of salt by digging away the sand even in the rough tracts between Egypt and Arabia, as it is also found as far as the oracle of Hammon

through the parched deserts of Africa, where at night it increases as the moon waxes. But the region of Cyrenaica too is famous for Hammoniac salt, itself so called because it is found under the sand. It is in colour like the alum called *schiston*, consisting of long opaque slabs, of an unpleasant flavour, but useful in medicine. That is most valued which is most transparent and splits into straight flakes. A remarkable feature is reported of it: of very little weight in its underground pits, when brought into the light of day it becomes incredibly heavy. The reason is obvious; the damp breath of the pits helps the workers by supporting the weight as does water. It is adulterated by the Sicilian salt I have said comes from the lake Cocanicus, as well as by Cypriot salt, which is wonderfully like it. In Hither Spain too at Egelesta salt is cut into almost transparent blocks; to this for some time past most physicians have given the first place among all kinds of salt.

4. "Every region in which salt is found is barren, and nothing will grow there. To speak generally, these remarks about the various kinds of native salt are comprehensive.

5. "Of artificial salt there are various kinds. The usual one, and the most plentiful, is made in salt pools by running into them sea water not without streams of fresh water, but rain helps very much, and above all much <warm> sunshine, without which it does not dry out. In Africa around Utica are formed heaps of salt like hills; when they have hardened under sun and moon, they are not melted by any moisture, and even iron cuts them with difficulty. It is also however made in Crete without fresh water by letting the sea flow into the pools, and around Egypt by the sea itself, which penetrates the soil, soaked as I believe it is, by the Nile. Salt is also made by pouring water from wells into salt pools. At Babylon the first condensation solidifies into a liquid bitumen like oil, which is also used in lamps. When this is taken away, salt is underneath. In Cappadocia too they bring water into salt pools from wells and a spring.

6. "In Chaonia there is a spring, from which they boil water, and on cooling obtain a salt that is insipid and not white.

7. "In the provinces of Gaul and Germany they pour salt water on burning logs. [In one part of the provinces of Spain they draw the brine from wells and call it *muria*.] The former indeed think that the wood used also makes a difference. The best is oak, for its pure ash by itself has the properties of salt; in some places hazel finds favour. So when brine is poured on it even wood turns into salt. Whenever wood is used in its making salt is dark. I find in Theophrastus that the Umbrians were wont to boil down in water the ash of reeds and rushes, until only a very little liquid remained. Moreover, from the liquor of salted foods salt is recovered by reboiling, and when evaporation is complete its saline character is regained. It is generally thought that the salt obtained from sardine brine is the most pleasant.

8. "Of sea salt the most in favour comes from Salamis in Cyprus, of pool salt that from Tarentum and that from Phrygia which is called Tattaean. The last two are useful for the eyes. The salt imported from Cappadocia in little bricks is said to impart a gloss to the skin. But the salt I have said comes from Citium smooths the skin better, and so after child-birth it is applied with melanthium to the abdomen.

9. "The saltest salt is the driest, the most agreeable and whitest of all is the Tarentine; for the rest, it is the whitest that is the most friable. All salt is made sweet by rain water, more agreeable, however, by dew, but plentiful by gusts of north wind. It does not form under a south wind. Flower of salt forms only with north winds. Tragasaean salt and Acanthian, so named after towns, neither crackles nor sputters in a fire, nor does froth of any salt, or scrapings, or powder. Salt of Agrigentum submits to fire and sputters in water. The colour too of salt varies: blushing red at Memphis, tawny red near the Oxus, purple at Centuripae, it is of such brightness near Gela (also in Sicily) that it reflects an image. In Cappadocia salt is quarried of a saffron colour, transparent, and very fragrant. For medicinal purposes the ancients used to favour most highly Tarentine salt, next, all kinds of sea salt, and of these especially that from foam, while for the eyes of draught animals and cattle salt of Tragasa and Baetica.

10. "To season meats and foods the most useful one melts easily and is rather moist, for it is less bitter, such as that of Attica and Euboea. For preserving meat the more suitable salt is sharp and dry, like that of Megara. A conserve too is made with fragrant additions, which is used as a relish, creating and sharpening an appetite for every kind of food, so that in innumerable seasonings it is the taste of salt that predominates, and it is looked for when we eat garum.

11. "Moreover sheep, cattle, and draught animals are encouraged to pasture in particular by salt; the supply of milk is much more copious, and there is even a far more pleasing quality in the cheese.

12. "Therefore, by Hercules, a civilized life is impossible without salt, and so necessary is this basic substance that its name is applied metaphorically even to intense mental pleasures. We call them *sales* (wit); all the humour of life, its supreme joyousness, and relaxation after toil, are expressed by this word more than by any other.

13. "It has a place in magistracies also and on service abroad, from which comes the term 'salary' (salt money); it had great importance among the men of old, as is clear from the name of the Salarian Way, since by it, according to agreement, salt was imported to the Sabines. King Ancus Marcius gave a largess to the people of 6,000 bushels of salt, and was the first to construct salt pools. Varro too is our authority that the men of old used salt as a relish, and that they ate salt with their bread is clear from a proverb. But the clearest proof of its importance lies in the fact that no sacrifice is carried out without the *mola salsa* (salted meal)." (Loeb translation, slightly adapted).

Several of these remarks have been discussed in the main text. Others of interest are these: the lack of vegetation around salt springs (4), its use as a preservative for foodstuffs (10), and its transport in "brick" form (8) or its formation into blocks (3). We are told that animals also need salt (11), and that it has a variety of medicinal uses (9). A number of places are mentioned, and one striking thing about these is their far-flung nature, from distant India to North Africa, as well as places nearer home in Italy and Sicily. There are also parts whose meaning is not very obvious, particularly that relating to "salt flower" (9).

Other relevant passages in Pliny include this:

> *"If more than a sextarius of salt is dropped into four sextarii of water, the water is saturated and the salt does not dissolve… [Such a solution] gives the strength and properties of the saltest sea"* (quoted by Healy 1999: 116, who points out that while the salinity of the oceans lies between 4 and 6 per cent, that of the Dead Sea is around 26%, very close to Pliny's figure here).

Aristotle (384-322 BC), *Meteorologica* II, iii. 359a.25 – b.4.

After explaining about salt solutions, and the properties of the Dead Sea, he says this:

> *"In Chaonia there is a spring of brackish water which flows into a neighbouring river that is sweet but contains no fish. For the inhabitants have a story that when Heracles, on his way through with the oxen from Erytheia, gave them the choice, they chose to get salt instead of fish from the spring. For they boil off some water from it and let the rest stand; and when it has cooled and the moisture has evaporated with the heat salt is left, not in lumps but in a loose powder like snow. It is also rather weaker than other salt and more of it must be used for seasoning, nor is it quite so white. Something of a similar sort happens also in Umbria. There is a place there where reeds and rushes grow: these they burn and throw their ashes into water and boil it till there is only a little left, and this when allowed to cool produces quite a quantity of salt"* (Loeb edition, 1952, trans. H.D.P. Lee).

Herodotus (ca 484-425 BC), *Histories* (IV. 181-5)

In describing the peoples and places of North Africa Herodotus has a lengthy presentation of the northern edge of the Sahara, i.e. inland "Libya". He refers to a series of "masses of great lumps of salt in hillocks", with springs of sweet water rising from them. The "peoples that dwell on the ridge as far as the Atlantes" have a mine of salt on it [the ridge] every ten days' journey, and men dwell there. Their houses are all built of the blocks of salt…. The salt there is both white and purple" (Loeb edition 1921, trans. A.D. Godley)

Livy (Titus Livius, 59 BC-AD 17), *History of Rome ("ab urbe condita")*

In 508 BC (AUC 246), at the time of the invasion of Rome by the Etruscans under Porsinna of Clusium, the senate gave "multa blandimenta" to the plebs: among these "the monopoly of salt, the price of which was very high, was taken out of the hands of individuals and wholly assumed by the government" (*History* II. IX. 6).

In 204 BC (AUC 550), during the Carthaginian Wars, the censors Marcus Livius and Gaius Claudius

> *"established a new revenue from the yearly production of salt. Both at Rome and throughout Italy salt was then sold at one-sixth of an as. The censors let contracts for the sale of salt at the same price at Rome, at a higher price even in market-towns and local centres, and at prices which varied from place to place. This source of revenue was generally believed to have been devised by only one of the censors, who was angry with the people because he had formerly been condemned by an unjust verdict; and that in the price of salt those tribes by whose efforts he had been condemned were most heavily burdened. Hence the cognomen Salinator was bestowed upon Livius"* (History XXIX. xxxvii. 3-4).

References

Aali, A., Abar, A., Boenke, N., Pollard, M., Rühli, F. & Stöllner, T. 2012a. Ancient salt mining and salt men: the interdisciplinary Chehrabad Douzlakh project in north-western Iran, *Antiquity* 86, Project gallery, http://antiquity.ac.uk/projgall/aali333/.

Aali, A., Stöllner, T., Abar, A. & Rühli, F. 2012b. The salt men of Iran: the salt mine of Douzlakh, Chehrabad, *Archäologisches Korrespondenzblatt* 42/1, 61-81.

Abarquero Moras, F.J. & Guerra Doce, E. (ed) 2010. *Los yacimientos de Villafáfila (Zamora) en el marco de las explotaciones salineras de la prehistoria europea*. Valladolid: Junta de Castilla y León, Consejería de Cultura y Turismo.

Abarquero Moras, F.J., Guerra Doce, E., Delibes de Castro, G., Palomino Lázaro, A.L. & Del Val Recio, J. 2010. Excavaciones en los "cocederos" de sal prehistóricos de Molino Sanchón II y Santioste (Villafáfila, Zamora). In: (ed) F. J. Abarquero Moras and E. Guerra Doce, *Los yacimientos de Villafáfila (Zamora) en el marco de las explotaciones salineras de la prehistoria europea*, 85-118. Valladolid: Junta de Castilla y León, Consejería de Cultura y Turismo.

Abarquero Moras, F.J., Guerra Doce, E., Delibes de Castro, G., Palomino Lázaro, A.L. & Del Val Recio, J. 2012. *Arqueología de la Sal en las Lagunas de Villafáfila (Zamora): Investigaciones sobre los cocederos prehistóricos*. Valladolid: Junta Castilla y León. Arqueología en Castilla y León, Monografías 9.

Adshead, S.A.M. 1992. *Salt and Civilisation*. Basingstoke & London: Macmillan.

Agricola, G. 1556. *De re metallica*. Basel: cum Privilegio Imperatoris in annos v & Galliarum Regis ad Sexennium (translation 1950 by H.C. Hoover, Dover Publications, New York).

Akridge, D.G. 2008. Methods for calculating brine evaporation rates during salt production, *Journal of Archaeological Science* 35, 1453-1462.

Alexianu, M., Dumitroaia, G. & Monah, D. 1992. Exploatarea surselor de apă sărată din Moldova: o abordare etnoarheologică, *Thraco-Dacica* 13/1-2, 159-167.

Alexianu, M. & Weller, O. 2007. Recherches ethnoarchéologiques sur le sel: les enquêtes de 2004 et les premiers résultats obtenus dans la zone de Poiana Slatinei à Lunca (dép. Neamţ, Roumanie). In: (ed) D. Monah, G. Dumitroaia, O. Weller and J. Chapman, *L'exploitation du sel à travers le temps*, 299-318. Piatra Neamţ: Editura Constantin Matasă.

Alexianu, M., Weller, O. & Brigand, R. 2007. *Izvoarele de apă sărată din Moldova subcarpatică. Cercetări etnoarheologice*. Iaşi: Casa Editorială Demiurg.

Alexianu, M., Weller, O. & Brigand, R. 2008. Usages et enjeux actuels autour des sources salées de Moldavie précarpatique, Roumanie. In: (ed) O. Weller, A. Dufraisse and P. Pétrequin, *Sel, eau et forêt. D'hier à aujourd'hui*, 49-72. Besançon: Presses universitaires de Franche-Comté. Collection "Les cahiers de la MSHE Ledoux", 12.

Alsop, G.I., Blundell, D.J. & Davison, I. (ed) 1996. *Salt Tectonics*. Geological Society Special Publication 100. London: The Geological Society.

Andronic, M. 1989. Cacica - un nou punct neolitic de exploatare a sării, *Studii și cercetări de istorie veche și arheologie* 40/2, 171-177.

Appadurai, A. 1986. Introduction: commodities and the politics of value. In: (ed) A. Appadurai, *The Social Life of Things: Commodities in cultural perspective*, 3-63. Cambridge: Cambridge University Press.

Arnold, D.E. 1985. *Ceramic Theory and Cultural Process*. Cambridge: Cambridge University Press.

Arthur, W.B. 2009. *The Nature of Technology. What it is and how it evolves*. London: Penguin Books.

Astrup, P., Bie, P. & Engell, H.C. 1993. *Salt and Water in Culture and Medicine*. Copenhagen: Munksgaard.

Ayanagüena Sanz, M. & Carnaval García, D. 2005. Sistemas de explotación de la sal en las Salinas de Espartinas. In: *Minería y metalurgia históricas en el sudoeste europeo*, 71-78. Madrid: SEDPGYM-SEHA.

Bailey, K.C. 1929. *The Elder Pliny's Chapters on Chemical Subjects. Part I*. London: Edward Arnold.

Bánffy, E. 2013. Tracing 6th-5th millennium BC salt exploitation in the Carpathian Basin. In: (ed) A. Harding and V. Kavruk, *Explorations in Salt Archaeology in the Carpathian Zone*, 201-207. Budapest: Archaeolingua.

Barth, F.E., Felber, H. & Schauberger, O. 1975. Radiokohlenstoffdatierung der prähistorischen Baue in den Salzbergwerken Hallstatt und Dürrnberg-Hallein, *Mitteilungen der anthropologischen Gesellschaft in Wien* 105, 45-52.

Bell, A., Gurney, D. & Healey, H. 1999. *Lincolnshire Salterns: Excavations at Helpringham, Holbeach St Johns and Bicker Haven*. Heckington (Sleaford): Heritage Trust of Lincolnshire. East Anglian Archaeology, Report 89.

Bell, M. 1990. *Brean Down Excavations 1983-1987*. London: English Heritage. English Heritage Archaeological Report 15.

Benac, A. 1978. Neke karakteristike neolitskih naselja u Bosni i Hercegnovi, *Materijali X. kongresa arheologa Jugoslavije (Prilep 1976)* 14, 15-26.

Bérest, P., Diamond, B., Duquesnoy, A., Durup, G., Feuga, B. & Lhoff, L. 2005. *Salt and brine production methods in France: main conclusions of the International Group of Experts (IEG) commissioned by the French regulatory authorities, Post-Mining Symposium, 16-17th November 2005, Nancy, France* (available at http://gisos.ensg.inpl-nancy.fr/post-mining-symposia/post-mining-2005/risk-management-and-socio-economic-impacts/).

Bergier, J.-F. 1982. *Une histoire du sel*. Fribourg: Office du Livre.

Bertaux, J.-P. 1976. L'archéologie du sel en Lorraine, 'Le briquetage de la Seille' (Etat actuel des recherches). In: (ed) J.-P. Millotte, A. Thévenin and B. Chertier, *Livret-Guide de l'excursion A7, Champagne, Lorraine, Alsace, Franche-Comté, UISPP IXe Congrès Nice 1976*, 64-79.

Bertaux, J.-P. 1977. Das Briquetage an der Seille in Lothringen, *Archäologisches Korrespondenzblatt* 7, 261-272.

Bettwieser, B. 2003. V. Die Grabungen 1997-98 (Parkstraße, Kolonnadenneubau) und 2001-2002 (Kurstraße 2, Gelände des ehemaligen Parkhotels). In: (ed) B. Kull, *Sole und Salz schreiben Geschichte*, 227-241. Mainz: von Zabern.

Biddulph, E., Foreman, S., Stafford, E., Stansbie, D. & Nicholson, R. 2012. *London Gateway. Iron Age and Roman salt making in the Thames Estuary. Excavation at Stanford Wharf Nature Reserve, Essex*. Oxford: Oxford Archaeology. Oxford Archaeology Monograph 18.

Blajer, W. 2001. *Skarby przedmiotów metalowych z epoki brązu i wczesnej epoki żelaza na ziemach polskich*. Kraków: Instytut Archeologii i Wydział Historyczny Uniwersytetu Jagiellońskiego w Krakowie.

Bloch, M.R. 1963. The social influence of salt, *Scientific American* 209, 89-98.

Bond, D. 1988. *Excavation at the North Ring, Mucking, Essex: a Late Bronze Age enclosure*. Chelmsford: Archaeology Section, Essex County Council. East Anglian Archaeology 43.

Bönisch, E. 1993. Briquetage aus bronzezeitlichen Gräbern der Niederlausitz, *Arbeits- und Forschungsberichte zur sächsischen Bodendenkmalpflege* 36, 67-84.

Borchert, H. & Muir, R.O. 1964. *Salt Deposits. The origin, metamorphism and deformation of evaporites*. London etc: Van Nostrand.

Boroffka, N.G.O. 2006. Resursele minerale din România și stadiul actual al cercetărilor privind mineritul preistoric, *Apulum* 43/1, 71-94.

Boroffka, N.G.O. 2009. Mineralische Rohstoffvorkommen und der Forschungsstand des urgeschichtlichen Bergbaues in Rumänien. In: (ed) M. Bartelheim and H. Stäuble, *Die wirtschaftlichen Grundlagen der Bronzezeit Europas / The Economic Foundations of the European Bronze Age*, 119-146. Rahden/Westf.: Verlag Marie Leidorf. Forschungen zur Archäometrie und Altertumswissenschaft, 4.

Bradley, R. 1975. Salt and settlement in the Hampshire Sussex borderland. In: (ed) K. W. De Brisay and K. A. Evans, *Salt: the study of an ancient industry*, 20-25. Colchester: Colchester Archaeological Group.

Braitsch, O. 1971. *Salt Deposits: their origin and composition*. Berlin-Heidelberg-New York: Springer-Verlag.

Bratu, O. 2009. *Depuneri de bronzuri între Dunărea mijlocie și Nistru în secolele XIII-VII a. Chr.* Bucharest: Renaissance.

Braunstein, J. & O'Brien, G.D. (ed) 1968. *Diapirism and Diapirs*. Tulsa: American Association of Petroleum Geologists, Memoir 8.

British Geological Survey 2006. *Mineral Planning Factsheet*. Available at www.bgs.ac.uk/downloads/start.cfm?id=1368, accessed 23 July 2013.

Britton, D. 1960. The Isleham hoard, Cambridgeshire, *Antiquity* 34, 279-82.

Brown, T.J., Shaw, R.A., Bide, T., Petavratzi, E., Raycraft, E.R. & Walters, A.S. 2013. *World Mineral Production 2007-11*. Keyworth, Nottingham: British Geological Survey.

Brysbaert, A. (ed) 2011. *Tracing Prehistoric Social Networks through Technology. A Diachronic Perspective on the Aegean*. Routledge Studies in Archaeology. London: Routledge.

Bukowski, K. 2013. Salt sources and salt springs in the Carpathian zone. In: (ed) A. Harding and V. Kavruk, *Explorations in Salt Archaeology in the Carpathian Zone*, 27-34. Budapest: Archaeolingua.

Bukowski, Z. 1963. O możliwości wykorzystywania solanek w okresie halsztackim na terenie Wielkopolski i Kujaw, *Archeologia Polski* 8/1, 246-273.

Bukowski, Z. 1985. Salt production in Poland in prehistoric times, *Archaeologia Polona* 24, 27-71.

Buzea, D. 2010. Experimentul ,Troaca', *Angustia* 14, 245-256.

Cappuccio, F. & Capewell, S. 2010. A sprinkling of doubt, *New Scientist* 1 May 2010, 22-3.

Cardale-Schrimpff, M. 1975. Prehistoric salt production in Colombia, South America. In: (ed) K. W. de Brisay and K. A. Evans, *Salt, the study of an ancient industry*, 84. Colchester: Colchester Archaeological Group.

Carozza, L., Marcigny, C. & Talon, M. 2009. Ordres et désordres de l'économie des sociétés durant l'Age du Bronze en France. In: (ed) M. Bartelheim and H. Stäuble, *Die wirtschaftlichen Grundlagen der Bronzezeit Europas / The Economic Foundations of the European Bronze Age*, 23-64. Rahden/Westf.: Verlag Marie Leidorf. Forschungen zur Archäometrie und Altertumswissenschaft, 4.

Carpentier, V., Ghesquière, E. & Marcigny, C. 2012. *Grains de Sel. Itinéraire dans les salines du littoral bas-normand de la préhistoire au XIXᵉ siècle*. Bayeux: Orep Éditions (revised edition; first edition published 2006 by Centre Régional d'Archéologie d'Alet and Association Manche Atlantique pour la Recherche Archéologique dans les Îles).

Carusi, C. 2008. *Il sale nel mondo greco (VI a.C.-III d.C.). Luoghi di produzione, circolazione commerciale, regimi di sfruttamento nel contesto del Mediterraneo antico*. Bari: Edipuglia. Pragmateiai.

Carvajal García, D., Tostón Menéndez, F.G. & Valiente Canovas, S. 2003. Las salinas espartinas (Ciempozuelos, Madrid): un ámbito de explotación de la sal desde la prehistoria. In: (ed) J. M. Mata-Perelló, *Libro de Actas del Primer Simposio Latino sobre Mineria, Metalurgia y Patrimonio Minero en el Area Mediterranea. Bellmunt del Priorat, 2002*, 53-62. La Pobla de Segur: Sociedad Española para la Defensa del Patrimonio Geológico y Minero (SEDPGYM) / Museu de Geologia de la UPC.

Cassola Guida, P. & Montagnari Kokelj, E. 2006. Produzione di sale nel golfo di Trieste: un'attività probabilmente antica. In: (ed) *Studi di protostoria in onore di Renato Peroni*, 327-332. Firenze: All'Insegna del Giglio.

Cavruc, V. & Chiricescu, A. (ed) 2006. *Sarea, Timpul și Omul*. Sfîntu Gheorghe: Editura Angustia.

Cavruc, V. & Harding, A. 2012. Prehistoric production and exchange of salt in the Carpathian-Danube region. In: (ed) V. Nikolov and K. Bacvarov, *Salt and Gold: the role of salt in prehistoric Europe*, 173-200. Provadia - Veliko Tarnovo: Verlag Faber.

Chapman, J. & Gaydarska, B. 2003. The provision of salt to Tripolye mega-sites. In: (ed) O. G. Korvin-Piotrovskiy, *Tripil'ski poselennya-giganti: Materiali mizhnarodnoy konferentsiy / Tripolian Settlements-Giants, the international symposium materials*, 203-211. Kiiv: Korvin Press.

Chintăuan, I. 2005. Pan used for salt extraction from brines, *Studii și Cercetări, Geologie-Geografie* 10, 75-78.

Chiricescu, A. 2013. *Civilizația tradițională a sării în estul Transilvaniei: raport de cercetare.* Sfîntu Gheorghe: Editura Angustia.

Chowne, P. 1978. Billingborough Bronze Age settlement: an interim note, *Lincolnshire History and Archaeology* 13, 15-21.

Chowne, P., Cleal, R.M.J., Fitzpatrick, A.P. & Andrews, P. 2001. *Excavations at Billingborough, Lincolnshire, 1975-8: a Bronze-Iron Age settlement and salt-working site.* Salisbury: Wessex Archaeology. East Anglian Archaeology Report 94.

Ciobanu, D. 2002. *Exploatarea sării în perioada marilor migrații (sec. I-XIII e.n.) în spațiul carpato-dunărean.* Buzău: Editura Alpha. Biblioteca Mousaios, 3.

Ciobanu, D. 2006. Exploatarea sării în spațiul Carpato-Dunărean în perioada post-romană și cea a marilor migrații. In: (ed) V. Cavruc and A. Chiricescu, *Sarea, Timpul și Omul,* 87-91. Sfântu Gheorghe: Editura Angustia.

Ciugudean, H. 2012. The chronology of the Gáva culture in Transylvania. In: (ed) W. Blajer, *Peregrinationes Archaeologicae in Asia et Europa Joanni Chochorowski dedicatae,* 107-121. Kraków: Instytut Archeologii Uniwersytetu Jagiellońskiego.

Ciugudean, H., Luca, S.A. & Georgescu, A. 2006. *Depozitul de Bronzuri de la Dipșa.* Sibiu: Muzeul Național Brukenthal. Bibliotheca Brukenthal, V.

Clark, J.G.D. 1952. *Prehistoric Europe: the economic basis.* London: Methuen.

Coffyn, A., Gomez, J. & Mohen, J.-P. 1981. *L'apogée de bronze atlantique: le dépôt de Vénat.* Paris: Picard. L'âge du bronze en France, 1.

Connah, G. 1991. The salt of Bunyoro: seeking the origins of an African kingdom, *Antiquity* 65, 479-494.

Cordier, G. 2009. *L'Âge du Bronze dans les pays de la Loire moyenne.* Joué-lès-Tours: Éditions la Simarre.

Cordier, G. & Bourhis, J.-R. 1996. *Le dépôt de l'âge du bronze final du Petit-Villatte à Neuvy-sur-Barangeon (Cher) et son contexte régional.* Sublaines (Joué-lès-Tours): Privately published.

Coutil, L. 1913. La cachette de fondeur de Larnaud (Jura), *9ᵉ Congrès préhistorique français, Compte rendu* 1913, 451-469.

Czapowski, G. & Bukowski, K. 2009. Złoża soli w Polsce - stan aktualny i perspektywy zagospodarowania, *Przegląd Geologiczny* 57, 798-811.

Czapowski, G. & Bukowski, K. 2010. Geology and resources of salt deposits in Poland: the state of the art, *Geological Quarterly* 54, 509-518.

Daire, M.-Y. 2003. *Le sel des Gaulois.* Paris: éditions errance. Collection des Hesperides.

Daire, M.-Y. (ed) 1994. *Le sel gaulois. Bouilleurs de sel et ateliers de briquetages armoricains à l'Âge du Fer.* Saint-Malo: Les Dossiers du Centre Régional d'Archéologie d'Alet, supplement Q.

de Brisay, K.W. & Evans, K.A. (ed) 1975. *Salt: the study of an ancient industry*. Colchester: Colchester Archaeological Group.

De Ceunynck, R. & Thoen, H. 1981. The Iron Age settlement at De Panne-Westhoek. Ecological and geological context, *Helinium* 21, 21-42.

De Leeuw, A., Bukowski, K., Krijgsman, W. & Kuiper, K.F. 2010. Age of the Badenian salinity crisis; impact of Miocene climate variability on the circum-Mediterranean region, *Geology* 38, 715-718.

De León, J.P. 2009. Rethinking the organization of Aztec salt production: a domestic perspective, *Archaeological Papers of the American Anthropological Association* 19(1), 45-57.

Deák, A. 2008. Mineritul tradițional al sării – o ocupație demult dispărută?, *Angustia* 12, 237-250.

Denton, D.A. 1984. *The Hunger for Salt. An anthropological, physiological and medical analysis*. Berlin-Heidelberg-New York-Tokyo: Springer-Verlag.

Desfossés, Y. (ed) 2000. *Archéologie préventive en Vallée de Canche. Les sites protohistoriques fouillés dans le cadre de la réalisation de l'Autoroute A.16*. Nord-Ouest Archéologie 11. Berck-sur-Mer: Centre de Recherches Archéologiques et de Diffusion Culturelle.

Di Fraia, T. 2011. Salt production and consumption in prehistory: toward a complex systems view. In: (ed) A. Vianello, *Exotica in the Prehistoric Mediterranean*, 26-32. Oxford: Oxbow Books.

Di Fraia, T. & Secoli, L. 2002. Il sito dell'età del bronzo di Isola di Coltano. In: (ed) N. Negroni Catacchio, *Atti Quinto Incontro di Studi di Preistoria e Protostoria in Etruria "Paesaggi d'acque"*, 79-93. Milan: Centro Studi di Preistoria e Archeologia.

Dopsch, H., Heuberger, B. & Zeller, K.W. (ed) 1994. *Salz (Salzburger Landesausstellung Hallein, Pernerinsel Keltenmuseum, 30. April bis 30. Oktober 1994)*. Salzburg: Salzburger Landesausstellungen.

Drăgănescu, L. 1997. *Originea sării și geneza masivelor de sare*. Ploiești: S.C. Grafica Prahoveană.

Duff, A.J., Ferguson, T.J., Bruning, S. & Whiteley, P. 2008. Salt woman and the twins, *Archaeology Southwest* 22/1, 6-7.

Ebenbichler, O.W. & Ebenbichler, M. 2009. *Tiroler Salz*. Hall in Tirol: Verlag Ablinger Garber.

Egg, M. 1985. *Die Hallstattzeitlichen Hügelgräber bei Helpfau-Uttendorf in Oberösterreich*. Mainz: Römisch-Germanisches Zentralmuseum.

Emons, H.-H. & Walter, H.-H. 1988. *Alte Salinen in Mitteleuropa. Zur Geschichte der Siedesalzerzeugung vom Mittelalter bis zur Gegenwart*. Leipzig: VEB Deutscher Verlag für Grundstoffindustrie.

Erdoğu, B., Özbaşaran, M., Erdoğu, R. & Chapman, J. 2003. Prehistoric salt exploitation in Tuz Gölü, central Anatolia: preliminary investigations, *Anatolia Antiqua* 11, 11-19.

Escacena Carrasco, J.L. 1994. Acerca de la producción de sal en el Neolítico Andaluz. In: (ed) M.J. Campos Carrasco, J.A. Pérez Maciás and F. Gómez, *Arqueología en el entorno del Bajo Guadiana*, 91-118. Huelva: Universidad de Huelva.

Escacena Carrasco, J.L., De Zuloaga Montesino, M.R. & Ladrón De Guevara Sánchez, I. 1996. *Guadalquivir salobre: elaboración prehistórica de sal marina en las antiguas bocas del río*. Sevilla: Confederación Hidrográfica del Guadalquivir.

Escacena Carrasco, J.L. & de Zuloaga Montesino, R. 1988. La Marismilla. ¿Una salina neolítica en el Bajo Guadalquivir?, *Revista de Arqueología* 9, 15-24.

Farrar, R.A.H. 1975. Prehistoric and Roman saltworks in Dorset. In: (ed) K. W. De Brisay and K. A. Evans, *Salt: the study of an ancient industry*, 14-20. Colchester: Colchester Archaeological Group.

Fawn, A.J., Evans, K.A., McMaster, I. & Davies, G.M.R. (ed) 1990. *The Red Hills of Essex: Salt-making in antiquity*. Colchester: Colchester Archaeological Group.

Figuls, A., Bonache, J., Aranda, J., Suñé, J., Vendrell, M., González, J., Mata-Perelló, J.M. & Sanz, J. 2007. Neolithic exploitation of halite at the "Val Salina" of Cardona (Catalonia, Spain). In: (ed) A. Figuls and O. Weller, *1a Trobada internacional d'arqueologia envers l'explotatió de la sal a la prehistòria i protohistòria, Cardona, 6-8 de desembre del 2003*, 199-218. Cardona: Institut de recerques envers la Cultura (IREC). Archaeologia Cardonensis 1.

Fíguls, A., Weller, O., Grandia, F., Bonache, J., González, J. & Lanaspa, R.M. 2013. La primera explotacion minera de la sal gema: la Vall Salina de Cardona (Cataluña, España), *Chungara, Revista de Antropología Chilena* 45, 177-195.

Figuls i Alonso, A. & Weller, O. (ed) 2007. *1a Trobada internacional d'arqueologia envers l'explotació de la sal a la prehistòria i protohistòria, Cardona 6-8 desembre del 2003*. Archaeologia Cardonensis I. Cardona: Institut de recerques envers la Cultura (IREC).

Fitts, R.L., Haselgrove, C., Lowther, P. & Willis, S. 1999. Melsonby revisited: survey and excavation 1992-95 at the site of discovery of the 'Stanwick' North Yorkshire hoard of 1843, *Durham Archaeological Journal* 14-15, 1-52.

Flad, R. 2011. *Salt Production and Social Hierarchy in Ancient China. An archaeological investigation of specialization in China's Three Gorges*. New York: Cambridge University Press.

Flad, R., Zhu, J., Wang, C., Chen, P., von Falkenhausen, L., Sun, Z. & Lin, S. 2005. Archaeological and chemical evidence for early salt production in China, *Proceedings of the National Academy of Sciences* 102 (35), 12618-12622.

Forbes, R.J. 1955. *Studies in Ancient Technology, vol. III*. Leiden: E.J. Brill.

Fraś, J.M. 2001. Zarys osadnictwa neolitycznego na terenie Wieliczki i okolicy, *Studia i materiały do dziejów żup solnych w Polsce* 21, 283-319.

Fries-Knoblach, J. 2001. *Gerätschaften, Verfahren und Bedeutung der eisenzeitlichen Salzsiederei in Mitteleuropa*. Leipzig: Professur für Ur- und Frühgeschichte der Universität Leipzig. Leipziger Forschungen zur ur- und frühgeschichtlichen Archäologie 2.

Gale, H.S. 1920. The potash deposits of Alsace. In: (ed) F. L. Ransome, H. S. Gale and E.F. Burchard, *Contributions to Economic Geology: Part I. - Metals and Non-Metals except Fuels*, 17-55. United States Geological Survey Bulletin 715.

García del Cura, M.A., Dabrio, C.J. & Ordóñez, S. 1996. Mineral resources of the Tertiary deposits of Spain. In: (ed) P. F. Friend and C. J. Dabrio, *Tertiary Basins of Spain: the stratigraphic record of crustal kinematics*, 26-40. Cambridge: Cambridge University Press. World and Regional Geology 6.

Gaydarska, B. 2003. Preliminary research on prehistoric salt exploitation in Bulgaria, *Dobrudzha* 21 (Isledvanya v chest na Henrieta Todorova), 110-122.

Gaydarska, B. & Chapman, J. 2007. Salt research in Bulgaria. In: (ed) D. Monah, G. Dumitroaia, O. Weller and J. Chapman, *L'exploitation du sel à travers le temps*, 147-160. Piatra-Neamț: Editura Constantin Matasă.

Giot, P.-R., L'Helgouach, J. & Briard, J. 1965. Le site du Curnic en Guisseny, *Annales de Bretagne* 72, 49-70.

Giovannini, A. 1985. Le sel et la fortune de Rome, *Athenaeum* 63, 373-387.

Godelier, M. 1969. La « monnaie de sel » des Baruya de Nouvelle-Guinée, *L'Homme* 9/2, 5-37.

Golovinsky, E. 2012. Das Kochsalz - Urgeschichte und Gegenwart einer bedeutenden Substanz. In: (ed) V. Nikolov and K. Bacvarov, *Salt and Gold: the role of salt in prehistoric Europe*, 333-340. Provadia & Veliko Tarnovo: Verlag Faber.

Good, C. 1995. Salt production and commerce in Guerrero, Mexico. An ethnographic contribution to historical reconstruction, *Ancient Mesoamerica* 6, 1-13.

Gosselain, O.P. 1992. Technology and style: potters and pottery among Bafia of Cameroon, *Man* 27/3, 559-586.

Gouletquer, P.L. 1969. Etudes sur les briquetages, IV, *Annales de Bretagne* 76, 119-147.

Gouletquer, P.L. 1970. *Les briquetages armoricains. Technologie protohistorique du sel en Armorique*. Rennes: Travaux du Laboratoire d'Anthropologie Préhistorique, Faculté des Sciences.

Gouletquer, P.L. 1975. Niger, country of salt. In: (ed) K. W. De Brisay and K. A. Evans, *Salt, the Study of an Ancient Industry*, 47-51. Colchester: Colchester Archaeological Group.

Gouletquer, P.L. & Kleinmann, D. 1984. Les salines du Manga (Niger). In: (ed) C. Lefébure and P. Lemonnier, *"Des choses dont la recherche est laborieuse...",* Paris: Maison des sciences de l'Homme. Techniques et Cultures. Bulletin de l'Equipe de Recherche 191, 3.

Grabner, M., Klein, A., Geihofer, D., Reschreiter, H., Barth, F.E., Sormaz, T. & Wimmer, R. 2007. Bronze age dating of timber from the salt-mine at Hallstatt, Austria, *Dendrochronologia* 24, 61-68.

Grabner, M., Reschreiter, H., Barth, F.E., Klein, A., Geihofer, D. & Wimmer, R. 2006. Dendrochronologie in Hallstatt, *Archäologie Österreichs* 17/1, 40-49.

Grabowska, M. 1967. Badania wykopaliskowe w Baryczy-Krzyszkowicach, pow. Kraków, na stanowisku VII, *Badania archeologiczne prowadzone przez Muzeum Żup Krakowskich Wieliczka w roku 1967*, 13-17.

Grassias, I. 2008. Les salines de Salins: un projet de restauration et de musée. In: (ed) O. Weller, A. Dufraisse and P. Pétrequin, *Sel, eau et forêt: D'hier à aujourd'hui*, 521-534. Besançon: Presses universitaires de Franche-Comté.

Guerra Doce, E., Delibes de Castro, G., Abarquero Moras, F.J., Del Val Recio, J. M. & Palomino Lázaro, A.L. 2011. The Beaker salt production centre of Molino Sanchón II, Zamora, Spain, *Antiquity* 85, 805-818.

Gurney, D. 1980. Evidence of Bronze Age salt-production at Northey, Peterborough, *Northants Archaeology* 15, 1-11.

Hansen, S. 1994. *Studien zu den Metalldeponierungen während der älteren Urnenfelderzeit zwischen Rhônetal und Karpatenbecken*. Bonn: Rudolf Habelt. Universitätsforschungen zur prähistorischen Archäologie, 21.

Harding, A. 1998. Resources and their distribution in the European Bronze Age. In: (ed) B. Hänsel, *Mensch und Umwelt in der Bronzezeit Europas*, 149-55. Kiel: Oetker-Voges Verlag.

Harding, A. 2000. *European Societies in the Bronze Age*. Cambridge: Cambridge University Press.

Harding, A. 2001. Natural resources as a factor in the evolution of Late Bronze Age groups in the Carpathian area. In: (ed) C. Kacsó, *Der nordkarpatische Raum in der Bronzezeit, Symposium Baia Mare 7-10 Oktober 1998*, 119-124. Baia Mare (Muzeul Judeţean Maramureş): Editura Cornelius. Biblioteca Marmatia I.

Harding, A. 2009. Producing salt in wooden troughs: the technology of Bronze Age salt production in Transylvania. In: (ed) G. Bodi, *In medias res praehistoriae. Miscellanea in honorem annos LXV peragentis Professoris Dan Monah oblata*, 195-204. Iaşi: Editura Universitaţii "Alexandru Ioan Cuza".

Harding, A. 2011. Evidence for salt production rediscovered in the Hungarian Central Mining Museum, *Antiquaries Journal* 91, 27-49.

Harding, A. & Kavruk, V. 2010. A prehistoric salt production site at Băile Figa, Romania, *Eurasia Antiqua* 16, 131-167.

Harding, A. & Kavruk, V. 2013. *Explorations in Salt Archaeology in the Carpathian Zone*. Budapest: Archaeolingua.

Healy, J.F. 1999. *Pliny the Elder on science and technology*. Oxford: Oxford University Press.

Hees, M. 1999. Vorgeschichtliche Salzgewinnung. Auf dem Spuren keltischer Salzsieder. In: (ed) C. Jacob, H. Spatz and S. Friederich, *Schliz - ein Schliemann im Unterland? 100 Jahre Archäologie im Heilbronner Raum (Ausstellungskatalog)*, 154-73. Heilbronn: Städtische Museen. Museo 14.

Hees, M. 2012. Die Bedeutung der vorgeschichtlichen Salzgewinnung in Südwestdeutschland. In: (ed) V. Nikolov and K. Bacvarov, *Salt and Gold: the role of salt in prehistoric Europe*, 277-286. Provadia & Veliko Tarnovo: Verlag Faber.

Hehn, V. n.d. [1873]. *Das Salz. Eine kulturhistorische Studie*. Leipzig [Berlin]: Insel-Verlag.

Hocquet, J.-C. 1986. L'évolution des techniques de fabrication du sel marin sur les rivages de l'Europe du Nord-Ouest (position des problèmes), *Revue du Nord* 1 spécial hors série, 3-22.

Hocquet, J.-C. 1994. Production et commerce du sel à l'Age du Fer et à l'époque romaine dans l'Europe du Nord-Ouest, *Revue du Nord* 76 (308), 9-20.

Hocquet, J.-C. 2001. *Hommes et Paysages du Sel. Une aventure millénaire*. Arles: Actes Sud.

Horiuchi, A., Ochiai, N., Kurozumi, H. & Miyata, Y. 2011. Detection of chloride from pottery as a marker for salt: a new analytical method validated using simulated salt-making pottery and applied to Japanese ceramics, *Journal of Archaeological Science* 38, 2949-2956.

Insoll, T.A. 2000. The road to Timbuktu: trade and empire. Camel caravans and the rise of commerce in medieval Mali, *Archaeology* 53/6, 48-52.

Jaanusson, H. & Jaanusson, V. 1988. Sea-salt as a commodity of barter in Bronze Age trade of northern Europe. In: (ed) B. Hardh, L. Larsson, D. Olausson and R. Petré, *Trade and Exchange in Prehistory. Studies in Honour of Berta Stjernquist*, 107-12. Lund: Historiska Museum. Acta Archaeologica Lundensia, series in 8°, 16.

Jenyon, M.K. 1986. *Salt Tectonics*. London & New York: Elsevier Applied Science Publishers.

Jockenhövel, A. 2012. Bronzezeitliche Sole in Mitteldeutschland: Gewinnung - Distribution - Symbolik. In: (ed) V. Nikolov and K. Bacvarov, *Salt and Gold: the role of salt in prehistoric Europe*, 239-257. Provadia / Veliko Tarnovo: Verlag Faber.

Jodłowski, A. 1968. Badania urządzeń solankowych kultury lendzelskiej w Baryczy, pow. Kraków, *Badania archeologiczne prowadzone przez Muzeum Żup Krakowskich Wieliczka w roku 1968*, 13-20.

Jodłowski, A. 1971. *Eksploatacja sóli na terenie Małopolski w pradziejach i we wczesnym średniowieczu*. Wieliczka: Muzeum Żup Krakowskich. Studia i materiały do dziejów żup sólnych w Polsce, 4.

Jodłowski, A. 1977. Die Salzgewinnung auf polnischen Boden in vorgeschichtlicher Zeit und im frühen Mittelalter, *Jahresschrift fur Mitteldeutsche Vorgeschichte* 61, 85-103.

Jones, M.U. 1977. Prehistoric salt equipment from a pit at Mucking, Essex, *Antiquaries Journal* 57, 317-19.

Jorns, W. 1960. Zur Salzgewinnung in Bad Nauheim während der Spätlatènezeit, *Germania* 38, 178-184.

Kacsó, C. 2009. Die Salz- und Erzvorkommen und die Verbreitung der bronzezeitlichen Metalldeponierungen in der Maramuresch. In: (ed) J. Gancarski, *Surowce naturalne w Karpatach oraz ich wykorzystanie w pradziejach i średniowieczu: materiały z konferencji, Krosno 25-26 listopada 2008 r.*, 341-372. Krosno: Muzeum Podkarpackie.

Kadrow, S. 2003. Charakterystyka technologiczna ceramiki kultury łużyckiej. In: (ed) S. Kadrow, *Kraków-Bieżanów, stanowisko 27 i Kraków-Rząka, stanowisko 1, osada kultury łużyckiej*, 205-220. Kraków: Zespół do Badań Autostrad. Via Archaeologica. Źródła z badań wykopaliskowych na trasie autostrady A4 w Małopolsce.

Kadrow, S. & Nowak-Włodarczak, E. 2003. Osada kultury łużyckiej na stan. 27 w Krakowie-Bieżanowie – organizacja warzelnictwa soli. In: (ed) J. Gancarski, *Epoka brązu i wczesna epoka żelaza w Karpatach polskich*, 549-567. Krosno: Muzeum Podkarpackie w Krośnie.

Kalicz, N. 2011. *Méhtelek. The First Excavated Site of the Méhtelek Group of the Early Neolithic Körös Culture in the Carpathian Basin*. Oxford: Archaeopress. BAR/ Archaeolingua, Central European Series 6.

Kalicz, N. 2012. Méhtelek-Nádas. The first excavated site of the Méhtelek fazies of the Early Neolithic Körös culture in the Carpathian Basin. In: (ed) A. Anders and Z. Siklósi, *The First Neolithic Sites in Central/South-East European Transect. Volume III. The Körös Culture in Eastern Hungary*, 113-123. BAR International Series 2334.

Kerger, P. 1999. Etude du matériel archéologique de l'atelier de sauniers à De Panne (Fl.-Occ.), *Lunula* 7, 74-81.

Kern, A., Kowarik, K., Rausch, A.W. & Reschreiter, H. (ed) 2009. *Kingdom of Salt. 7000 years of Hallstatt* (English version of *Salz-Reich. 7000 Jahre Hallstatt*, 2008). Veröffentlichungen der prähistorischen Abteilung 3. Vienna: Naturhistorisches Museum.

Kinory, J. 2012. *Salt Production, Distribution and Use in the British Iron Age*. Oxford: Archaeopress. BAR British Series 559.

Kobal', J.V. 1992. Khronologiya skarbiv piznogo bronzovogo viku prikarpattya, *Novi Materyali z Arkheologyi Prikarpattya i Voliny* 2, 30-32.

Kopaka, K. & Chaniotakis, N. 2003. Just taste additive? Bronze Age salt from Zakros, Crete, *Oxford Journal of Archaeology* 22/1, 53-66.

Kopytoff, I. 1986. The cultural biography of things: commoditization as process. In: (ed) A. Appadurai, *The Social Life of Things: Commodities in Cultural Perspective*, Cambridge: Cambridge University Press.

Kowarik, K. 2009. Aus nah und fern. Gedanken zu den Versorgungsstrukturen des bronzezeitlichen Salzbergbaus in Hallstatt, *Mitteilungen der anthropologischen Gesellschaft in Wien* 139, 105-113.

Kowarik, K. & Reschreiter, H. 2010. Provisioning a salt mine. On the infrastructure of the Bronze Age salt mines of Hallstatt. In: (ed) F. Mandl and H. Stadler, *Archäologie in den Alpen. Alltag und Kult*, 105-116. Haus im Ennstal: ANISA, Verein für alpine Forschung. Forschungsbericht der ANISA Band 3 / Nearchos Band 19.

Kowarik, K. & Reschreiter, H. 2011. Hall-Impact. Disentangling climate and culture impact on the prehistoric salt mines of Hallstatt (Austria). In: (ed) C. Gutjahr and G. Tiefengraber, *Beiträge zur Mittel- und Spätbronzezeit sowie zur Urnenfelderzeit am Rande der Südostalpen*, 241-256. Rahden/Westf.: Marie Leidorf Verlag. Internationale Archäologie. Arbeitsgemeinschaft, Symposium, Tagung, Kongress 15.

Kull, B. 2003a. I. Die Erforschung der Salinenareale seit 1837. In: (ed) B. Kull, *Sole und Salz schreiben Geschichte*, 95-206. Mainz: von Zabern.

Kull, B. (ed) 2003b. *Sole und Salz schreiben Geschichte. 50 Jahre Landesarchäologie: 150 Jahre Archäologische Forschung in Bad Nauheim.* Archäologische und Paläontologische Denkmalpflege, Landesamt für Denkmalpflege Hessen. Mainz: von Zabern.

Kurlansky, M. 2002. *Salt, a World History.* London: Jonathan Cape.

Kytlicová, O. 2007. *Jungbronzezeitliche Hortfunde in Böhmen.* Stuttgart: Franz Steiner Verlag. Prähistorische Bronzefunde, Abt. XX, Band 12.

Lane, T. & Morris, E.L. (ed) 2001. *A Millennium of Saltmaking: prehistoric and Romano-British salt production in the Fenland.* Lincolnshire Archaeology and Heritage Reports Series, 4. Sleaford: Heritage Trust of Lincolnshire.

Lauermann, E. & Rammer, E. 2013. *Die urnenfelderzeitlichen Metallhortfunde Niederösterreichs. Mit besonderer Berücksichtigung der zwei Depotfunde aus Enzersdorf im Thale.* Bonn: Rudolf Habelt. Universitätsforschungen zur prähistorischen Archäologie 226.

Laumann, H. 2000. Hallstattzeitliche Salzsiederei in Werl. In: (ed) H. G. Horn, H. Hellenkemper, G. Isenberg and H. Koschik, *Millionen Jahre Geschichte, Fundort Nordrhein-Westfalen. Begleitbuch zur Landesausstellung*, 250-251. Mainz: von Zabern.

Lazarovici, G. & Lazarovici, C.-M. 2011. Some salt sources in Transylvania and their connections with the archaeological sites in the area. In: (ed) M. Alexianu, O. Weller and R.-G. Curca, *Archaeology and anthropology of salt. Proceedings of the International Colloquium, 1-5 October 2008. Al. I. Cuza University (Iaşi, Romania)*, 89-110. Oxford: Archaeopress. British Archaeological Reports, International Series 2198.

Lazarovici, G. & Maxim, Z. 1995. *Gura Baciului.* Cluj-Napoca: Muzeul Naţional de Istorie a Transilvaniei.

Leech, R.H. 1977. Late Iron Age and Romano-British briquetage sites at Quarrylands Lane, Badgworth, *Somerset Archaeology and Natural History* 121, 89-96.

Leech, R.H. 1981. The Somerset Levels in the Romano-British period. In: (ed) T. Rowley, *The Evolution of Marshland Landscapes: papers presented to a conference on marshland landscapes held in Oxford in December 1979*, 20-51. Oxford: Oxford University, Department for External Studies.

Leidinger, W. 1983. Frühe Salzgewinnung in Werl, Kreis Soest, Westfalen, *Archäologisches Korrespondenzblatt* 13, 269-74.

Leidinger, W. 1996. Salzgewinnung an den Solquellen der Saline Werl. In: (ed) R. Just and U. Meissner, *Das Leben in der Saline - Arbeiter und Unternehmer*, 189-215. Halle/Saale: Technisches Halloren- und Salinemuseum. Schriften und Quellen zur Kulturgeschichte des Salzes 3 (also separately published as a pamphlet, 27 pp.).

Leman-Delerive, G., Gautier, A. & Calonne, E. 1996. Bray-Dunes: habitat et industrie du sel à la fin de l'Age du Fer, *Revue du Nord* 78, 15-43.

Lemonnier, P. 1993. Introduction. In: (ed) P. Lemonnier, *Technological Choices. Transformation in material cultures since the Neolithic*, 1-35. London & New York: Routledge.

Levy, J. 1982. *Social and Religious Organization in Bronze Age Denmark. An analysis of ritual hoard finds.* Oxford: British Archaeological Reports. BAR International Series 124.

Lofty, G.J., Hillier, J.A., Bate, D.G., Linley, K.A. & Hutchinson, N.E. 1994. *World Mineral Statistics 1988-92. Production: Exports: Imports.* Keyworth, Nottingham: British Geological Survey.

Louwe Kooijmans, L.P., van den Broeke, P.W., Fokkens, H. & van Gijn, A.L. (ed) 2005. *The Prehistory of the Netherlands.* Amsterdam: Amsterdam University Press.

Lovejoy, P.E. 1986. *Salt and the Desert Sun: A history of salt production and trade in Central Sudan.* Cambridge: Cambridge University Press.

Lunar, R., Moreno, T., Lombardero, M., Reguero, M., López-Vera, F., Martínez del Olmo, W., Mallo García, J.M., Saenz de Santa Maria, J.A., García-Palomero, F., Higueras, P., Ortega, L. & Capote, R. 2002. Economic and environmental geology. In: (ed) W. Gibbons and T. Moreno, *The Geology of Spain*, 473-510. London: The Geological Society.

MacGregor, G. & De Wardener, H.E. 1998. *Salt, Diet and Health: Neptune's poisoned chalice.* Cambridge: Cambridge University Press.

Manem, S. 2010. Des habitats aux sites de rassemblement à vocation rituelle. L'âge du Bronze selon le concept de «chaîne opératoire», *Les Nouvelles de l'archéologie* 2010, 30-36.

Marc, D. 2006. Sisteme de transport şi de comercializare tradiţională a sării. In: (ed) V. Cavruc and A. Chiricescu, *Sarea, Timpul şi Omul*, 152-157. Sfântu Gheorghe: Editura Angustia.

Marcigny, C. & Le Goaziou, E. 2012. Coastal salt for preserving and eating. In: (ed) A. Lehoërff, *Beyond the Horizon. Societies of the Channel and North Sea 3,500 years ago*, 101. Paris: Somogy Art Publishers / BOAT 1550 BC.

Marro, C. 2010. Where did Late Chalcolithic Chaff-Faced Ware originate ? Cultural dynamics in Anatolia and Transcaucasia at the dawn of urban civilization (ca. 4500-3500 BC), *Paléorient* 36/2, 35-55.

Marro, C. 2011. La mine de sel de Duzdaği: une exploitation plurimillénaire, *Mission Archéologique du Bassin de l'Araxe & Academy of Sciences of Azerbaijan, Naxçivan branch (AMEA)* http://www.clio.fr/securefilesystem/Marro-Clio2011-texte.doc, accessed 29 April 2013.

Marro, C., Bakhshaliyev, V. & Sanz, S. 2010. Archaeological investigations on the salt mine of Duzdaği (Nakhchivan, Azerbaïdjan), *TÜBA-AR* 13, 229-244.

Matshetshe, K. 2001. Salt production and salt trade in the Makgadikgadi pans, *Pula, Botswana Journal of African Studies* 15/1, 75-90.

Matthias, W. 1961. Das mitteldeutsche Briquetage - Formen, Verbreitung und Verwendung, *Jahresschrift für mitteldeutsche Vorgeschichte* 45, 119-225.

Matthias, W. 1976. Die Salzproduktion - ein bedeutender Faktor in der Wirtschaft der frühbronzezeitlichen Bevölkerung an der mittleren Saale, *Jahresschrift für mitteldeutsche Vorgeschichte* 60, 373-94.

Maxim, Z. 1999. *Neo-Eneoliticul din Transilvania*. Cluj-Napoca: Muzeul Naţional de Istorie Transilvaniei. Biblioteca Musei Napocensis 19.

McGovern, P.E. & Notis, M.R. (ed) 1989. *Cross-Craft and Cross-Cultural Interactions in Ceramics*. Ceramics and Civilization IV. Westerville, OH: American Ceramic Society.

McKillop, H. 2002. *Salt: White Gold of the Ancient Maya*. Gainesville: University Press of Florida.

Mollat, M. (ed) 1968. *Le rôle du sel dans l'histoire*. Paris: Presses Universitaires de France.

Monah, D. 2002. L'exploitation préhistorique du sel dans les Carpathes orientales. In: (ed) O. Weller, *Archéologie du sel: techniques et sociétés dans la pré- et protohistoire européenne / Salzarchäologie. Techniken und Gesellschaft in der Vor- und Frühgeschichte Europas*, 135-146. Rahden/Westf.: Verlag Marie Leidorf.

Monah, D., Dumitroaia, G., Weller, O. & Chapman, J. (ed) 2007. *L'exploitation du sel à travers le temps*. Piatra Neamţ: Editura Constantin Matasă.

Montagnari Kokelj, E. 2007. Salt and the Trieste karst (north-eastern Italy). In: (ed) D. Monah, G. Dumitroaia, O. Weller and J. Chapman, *L'exploitation du sel à travers le temps*, 161-189. Piatra-Neamţ: Editura Constantin Matasă.

Mordant, C., Mordant, D. & Prampart, J.-Y. 1976. *Le dépôt de bronze de Villethierry (Yonne)*. Paris: CNRS. IXᵉ supplément à Gallia Préhistoire.

Morère, N. 2002. À propos du sel hispanique. In: (ed) O. Weller, *Archéologie du sel: techniques et sociétés dans la pré- et protohistoire européenne / Salzarchäologie. Techniken und Gesellschaft in der Vor- und Frühgeschichte Europas*, 183-188. Rahden/Westf.: Verlag Marie Leidorf. Internationale Archäologie: Arbeitsgemeinschaft, Symposium, Tagung, Kongress, Band 3.

Morin, D. 2002. L'extraction du sel dans les Alpes durant la Préhistoire. La source salée de Moriez, Alpes de Haute Provence (France) (cal. BC 5810-5526). In: (ed) O. Weller, *Archéologie du sel: techniques et sociétés dans la pré- et protohistoire européenne / Salzarchäologie. Techniken und Gesellschaft in der Vor- und Frühgeschichte Europas*, 153-162. Rahden/Westf.: Verlag Marie Leidorf.

Morin, D., Lavier, C. & Guiomar, M. 2006. The beginnings of salt extraction in Europe (sixth millennium BC): the salt spring of Moriez (Alpes-de-Haute-Provence, France), *Antiquity* 80 Project Gallery, http://antiquity.ac.uk/ProjGall/morin/index.html, accessed 24/10/2006.

Morris, E.L. 1985. Prehistoric salt distributions: two case studies from western Britain, Bulletin Board of Celtic Studies 32, 336-79.

Morris, E.L. 1994. Production and distribution of pottery and salt in Iron Age Britain: a review, Proceedings of the Prehistoric Society 60, 371-94.

Morris, E.L. 2007. Making magic: later prehistoric and early Roman salt production in the Lincolnshire Fenland. In: (ed) C. Haselgrove and T. Moore, *The Later Iron Age in Britain and Beyond*, 430-443. Oxford: Oxbow Books.

Much, M. 1902. Prähistorischer Bergbau in den Alpen, *Zeitschrift des deutschen und österreichischen Alpenvereins* 33, 1-31.

Müller, D.W. 1987. Neolithisches Briquetage von der mittleren Saale, *Jahresschrift für mitteldeutsche Vorgeschichte* 70, 135-52.

Müller, D.W. 1988. Die Kochsalzgewinnung in der Urgeschichte des Mittelelbe-Saale-Raumes. In: (ed) B. Gediga, *Surowce mineralne w pradziejach i we wczesnym średniowieczu Europy środkowej*, 91-105. Wrocław etc: Zakład Narodowy Imienia Ossolińskich, Wydawnictwo Polskiej Akademii Nauk. Prace Komisji Archeologicznej / Polska Akademia Nauk, Oddział we Wrocławiu, 6.

Müller, D.W. 1996. Die ur- und frühgeschichtliche Salzgewinnung in Mitteldeutschland. Zeugnisse und Auswirkungen. In: (ed) R. Just and U. Meissner, *Das Leben in der Saline - Arbeiter und Unternehmer. Internationale Salzgeschichtetagung*, 177-188. Halle: Technisches Halloren- und Salinemuseum. Schriften und Quellen zur Kulturgeschichte des Salzes, 3.

Multhauf, R.P. 1978. *Neptune's Gift. A history of common salt*. Baltimore: John Hopkins University Press. John Hopkins Studies in the History of Technology, new series 2.

Nave, A. 2010. Salt trade. In: (ed) K. A. Appiah and H. L. Gates, *Encyclopedia of Africa*, 345-6. New York: Oxford University Press.

Nenquin, J.A.E. 1961. *Salt. A Study in Economic Prehistory*. Gent: De Tempel. Dissertationes Archaeologicae Gandenses, 6.

Nijboer, A.J., Attema, P.A.J. & Van Oortmerssen, G.J.M. 2005/2006. Ceramics from a Late Bronze Age saltern on the coast near Nettuno (Rome, Italy), *Palaeohistoria* 47/48, 141-205.

Nikolov, V. 2012. Salt, early complex society, urbanization: Provadia-Solnitsata (5500-4200 BC). In: (ed) V. Nikolov and K. Bacvarov, *Salt and Gold: the role of salt in prehistoric Europe*, 11-65. Provadia/Veliko Tarnovo: Verlag Faber.

Nikolov, V. (ed) 2008. *Praistoricheski solodobiven tsentr Provadiya-Solintsata. Razkopki 2005-2007 g.* Sofia: Bl'garska Akademiya na Naukite / Natsionalen Arkheologicheski Institut i Muzej.

Nikolov, V. (ed) 2009. *Provadiya-Solintsata. Arkheologicheski razkopki i izsledvaniya prez 2008 g. Predvaritelen otchet.* Sofia: Publisher not stated.

Nikolov, V. (ed) 2010. *Solta e Zlato. Praistoricheski solodobiven tsentr Provadiya-Solnitsata.* Sofia: B'lgarska Akademiya na Naukite / Natsionalen Arkheologicheski Institut s Muzej / Istoricheski Muzej - Provadiya.

Nitta, E. 1997. Iron-smelting and salt-making industries in northeast Thailand, *Indo-Pacific Prehistory Association Bulletin* 16 (Chiang Mai Papers 3), 153-160.

Olivier, L. 2000 (2001). Le «Briquetage de la Seille» (Moselle): nouvelles recherches sur une exploitation proto-industrielle du sel à l'Age du Fer, *Antiquités nationales* 32, 143-71.

Olivier, L. 2005. Le «Briquetage de la Seille» (Moselle): bilan d'un programme de cinq années de recherches archéologiques (2001-2005), *Antiquités nationales* 37, 219-230.

Olivier, L. 2007. Les «maîtres du sel» celtiques et gaulois de la vallée de la Seille (Moselle), *Le pays lorrain* March 2007 no. 1, 5-14.

Olivier, L. 2010. Nouvelles recherches sur le site de sauniers du premier Age du Fer de Marsal «La Digue» (Moselle), *Antiquités nationales* 41, 127-160.

Olivier, L. & Kovacik, J. 2006. The 'Briquetage de la Seille': proto-industrial salt production in the European Iron Age, *Antiquity* 80, 558-566.

Palmer-Brown, C. 1993. Bronze Age salt production at Tetney, *Current Archaeology* 136, 143-45.

Pany, D. & Teschler-Nicola, M. 2007. Working in a salt mine: everyday life for the Hallstatt females?, *Lunula* 15, 89-97.

Pasquinucci, M. & Menchelli, S. 2002. The Isola di Coltano Bronze Age village and the salt production in north coastal Tuscany (Italy). In: (ed) O. Weller, *Archéologie du sel: techniques et sociétés dans la pré- et protohistoire européenne / Salzarchäologie. Techniken und Gesellschaft in der Vor- und Frühgeschichte Europas*, 177-182. Rahden/Westf.: Marie Leidorf. Internationale Archäologie 3.

Peacock, D.P.S. 1981. Archaeology, ethnology, and ceramic production. In: (ed) H. Howard and E. L. Morris, *Production and Distribution: a ceramic viewpoint*, 187-94. Oxford: British Archaeological Reports, International Series 120.

Pétrequin, P., Pétrequin, A.-M. & Weller, O. 2000. Cuire la pierre et cuire le sel en Nouvelle-Guinée: des techniques actuelles de régulation sociale. In: (ed) P. Pétrequin, P. Fluzin, J. Thiriot and P. Benoit, *Arts du feu et productions artisanales*, 545-564. Antibes: Éditions APDCA. XXᵉ Rencontres Internationales d'Archéologie et d'Histoire d'Antibes.

Pétrequin, P. & Weller, O. 2007. XVᵉ siècle av. J.-C.: la reprise de la croissance démographique dans le Jura. In: (ed) H. Richard, M. Magny and C. Mordant, *Emprises, déprises et rythmes agricoles à l'Age du Bronze. Actes du Colloque CTHS Besançon 2004*, 197-210. Paris: Editions du CTHS. Documents préhistoriques du CTHS, 21.

Pétrequin, P., Weller, O., Gauthier, É., Dufraisse, A. & Piningre, J.-F. 2001. Salt springs exploitation without pottery during prehistory. From New Guinea to the French Jura. In: (ed) S. Beyries and P. Pétrequin, *Ethno-Archaeology and its Transfers*, 37-65. Oxford: BAR International Series 983.

Petzel, M. 1987. Briquetage-Funde im Bezirk Cottbus, *Ausgrabungen und Funde* 32, 62-66.

Poncelet, L. 1966. Le briquetage de la Seille, *Bulletin Association des amis de l'archéologie Mosellane* 1966/4, 1-15.

Potts, D. 1984. On salt and salt gathering in ancient Mesopotamia, *Journal of the Economic and Social History of the Orient* 27(3), 225-271.

Preier, H. 1997 [1999]. Den Salzsiedern auf dem Spur, *Archäologie aktuell Sachsen* 5, 134-9.

Prilaux, G. 2000. *La production de sel à l'Age du Fer. Contribution à l'établissement d'une typologie à partir des exemples de l'autoroute A16.* Montagnac: éditions monique mergoil. Protohistoire européene 5.

Prilaux, G., Chaidron, C., Lemaire, F. & Masse, A. 2011. Les âges du sel en Gaule du Nord, *Archéopages* 31 (January), 22-31.

Primas, M. 1997. Bronze Age economy and ideology: Central Europe in focus, *Journal of European Archaeology* 5, 115-130.

Proctor, J. 2012. The Needles Eye enclosure, Berwick-upon-Tweed, *Archaeologia Aeliana* 5th series 41, 19-122.

Pryor, F. 1980. *Excavation at Fengate, Peterborough, England: the Third Report.* Northants Archaeol. Soc., Monograph 1 / Royal Ontario Museum, Archaeol. Monograph 6.

Rau, V. 1968. Les courants du trafic du sel portugais du XIVe au XVIIIe siècle. In: (ed) M. Mollat, *Le rôle du sel dans l'histoire*, 53-71. Paris: Presses Universitaires de France.

Reina, R.E. & Monaghan, J. 1981. The ways of the Maya. Salt production in Sacapulas, Guatemala, *Expedition* 23, 13-33.

Renfrew, C. 1986. Varna and the emergence of wealth in prehistoric Europe. In: (ed) A. Appadurai, *The Social Life of Things: Commodities in cultural perspective*, 141-168. Cambridge: Cambridge University Press.

Reyman, T.S. 1934. Badania terenowe na polu "Karasiniec" w Pobiedniku Wielkim pow. Miechów, *Materiały prehistoryczne* 1, 29-58.

Riehm, K. 1954. Vorgeschichtliche Salzgewinnung an Saale und Seille, *Jahresschrift für mitteldeutsche Vorgeschichte* 38, 112-56.

Riehm, K. 1961. Prehistoric salt-boiling, *Antiquity* 35, 181-91.

Riehm, K. 1962. Werkanlagen und Arbeitsgeräte urgeschichtlicher Salzsieder, *Germania* 40, 360-400.

Riera, P., de Sal, M., Sala i Queralt, M., Galera i Pedrosa, A., Fuentes i Martínez, A., Arnau i Reig, R., Cardona i Oliván, F., Daura i Jorba, A., Vendrell i Manent, M., Barberà i Soler, J. & Martínez i Muñoz, D. 2001. *La Sal.* Cardona: Patronat Municipal de Museus.

Rios, J.M. 1968. Saline deposits of Spain. In: (ed) R. B. Mattox, *Saline Deposits: a symposium based on papers from the International Conference on Saline Deposits, Houston, Texas, 1962*, 59-74. New York: Geological Society of America, Special Papers 88.

Roux, V. 2010. Lecture anthropologique des assemblages céramiques. Fondements et mise en œuvre de l'analyse technologique, *Les Nouvelles de l'archéologie* 119, 4-9.

Roymans, N. 1991. Late Urnfield societies in the northwest European plain and the expanding networks of Central European Hallstatt groups. In: (ed) N. Roymans and F. Theuws, *Images of the Past: Studies on ancient societies in northwestern Europe*, 9-89. Amsterdam: Instituut voor Prae- en Protohistorische Archeologie Albert Egges van Giffen. Studies in Prae- en Protohistorie 7.

Rusu, M. 1963. Die Verbreitung der Bronzehorte in Transsilvanien vom Ende der Bronzezeit bis in die mittlere Hallstattzeit, *Dacia* 7, 177-210.

Rusu, M. 1981. Bemerkungen zu den grossen Werkstätten- und Giessereifunden aus Siebenbürgen. In: (ed) H. Lorenz, *Studien zur Bronzezeit. Festschrift für Wilhelm Albert v. Brunn*, 375-402. Mainz: v. Zabern.

Saile, T. 2000. Salz im ur- und frühgeschichtlichen Mitteleuropa - eine Bestandsaufnahme, *Bericht der Römisch-Germanischen Kommission* 81, 129-234.

Saile, T. 2012. Salt in the Neolithic of Central Europe: production and distribution. In: (ed) V. Nikolov and K. Bacvarov, *Salt and Gold: the role of salt in prehistoric Europe*, 225-238. Provadia & Veliko Tarnovo: Verlag Faber.

Salaš, M. 2005. *Bronzové depoty střední až pozdní doby bronzové na Moravě a ve Slezsku*. Brno: Moravské zemské muzeum.

Santley, R.S. 2004. Prehistoric salt production at El Salado, Veracruz, Mexico, *Latin American Antiquity* 15(2), 199-221.

Scachetti, E. 2008. La saline d'Arc-et-Senans: le sel, l'eau et le bois. In: (ed) O. Weller, A. Dufraisse and P. Pétrequin, *Sel, eau et forêt: D'hier à aujourd'hui*, 505-519. Besançon: Presses universitaires de Franche-Comté.

Schachner, A. 2004. Salz und Salzgewinnung im antiken Iran. In: (ed) T. Stöllner, *Katalog zur Iran-Ausstellung des Bergbau-Museum Bochum*, 518-525. Bochum: Deutsches Bergbau-Museum.

Schleiden, M.J. 1875. *Das Salz. Seine Geschichte, seine Symbolik und seine Bedeutung im Menschenleben. Eine monographische Skizze*. Leipzig: Wilhelm Engelmann. Dokumente zur Geschichte von Naturwissenschaft, Medizin und Technik, 6.

Schliz, A. 1903. Salzgewinnung in der Hallstattzeit mit Bezugnahme auf die mutmasslichen Verhältnisse in Württembergisch-Franken, *Zeitschrift für Ethnologie* 35, 642-650.

Schmidt, J. 1894. Cylinder und andere Thon-Gebilde unbekannten Gebrauchs aus der Umgegend von Halle a.S., *Mittheilungen aus dem Provincial-Museum der Provinz Sachsen zu Halle an der Saale* 1, 48-59.

Schroeter, J. 1943. Das Salz in der Vorgeschichte und in der Antike, *Ciba-Zeitschrift* 8, 3154-3160.

Schwaiger, B. 1977. *Wie kommt das Salz ins Meer?* Wien & Hamburg: Paul Zsolnay.

Sealey, P.R. 1995. New light on the salt industry and red hills of prehistoric and Roman Essex, *Essex Archaeology and History* 26, 65-81.

Shennan, S. 1993. Commodities, transactions and growth in the Central European Early Bronze Age, *Journal of European Archaeology* 1/2, 59-72.

Sherlock, R.L. 1921. *Rock-Salt and Brine*. London: HMSO. Memoirs of the Geological Survey: Special Reports on the Mineral Resources of Great Britain, vol. XVIII.

Sherlock, S.J. & Vyner, B. 2013. Iron Age saltworking on the Yorkshire coast at Street House, Loftus, Cleveland, *Yorkshire Archaeological Journal* 85, 46–67.

Silverman, B.W. 1998. *Density Estimation for Statistics and Data Analysis*. London: Chapman and Hall.

Simon, T. 1995. *Salz und Salzgewinnung im nördlichen Baden-Württemberg. Geologie-Technik-Geschichte*. Sigmaringen: Jan Thorbecke Verlag. Forschungen aus Württembergisch Franken, 42.

Simons, A. 1987. Archäologischer Nachweis eisenzeitlichen Salzhandels von der Nordseeküste ins Rheinland, *Archäologische Informationen* 10, 8-14.

Ślączka, A. & Oszczypko, N. 2002. Paleogeography of the Badenian salt basin (Carpathian foredeep, Poland and Ukraine), *Geologica Carpathica* 53 (Special Issue: Proceedings of XVII. Congress of Carpathian-Balkan Geological Association, Bratislava, September 1st - 4th 2002), 1-8 http://www.geologicacarpathica.sk/special/S/Slaczka_Oszczypko.pdf.

Smith, R.A. 1918. Red Hills as salt-works, *Proceedings of the Society of Antiquaries of London* 30, 36-54.

Sprockhoff, E. 1930. *Zur Handelsgeschichte der germanischen Bronzezeit*. Berlin: de Gruyter. Vorgeschichtliche Forschungen, 7.

Stoica, C. & Gherasie, I. 1981. *Sarea și sărurile de potasiu și magneziu din România*. Bucharest: Editura Tehnică.

Stöllner, T. 1999. *Der prähistorische Salzbergbau am Dürrnberg bei Hallein I. Forschungsgeschichte - Forschungsstand - Forschungsanliegen*. Rahden/Westf.: Verlag Marie Leidorf. Dürrnberg-Forschungen Band 1, Abteilung Bergbau.

Stöllner, T. 2002. *Der prähistorische Salzbergbau am Dürrnberg bei Hallein II. Die Funde und Befunde der Bergwerksausgrabungen zwischen 1990 und 2000*. Rahden/Westf.: Verlag Marie Leidorf. Dürrnberg-Forschungen Band 3, Abteilung Bergbau; Veröffentlichungen aus dem Deutschen Bergbau-Museum Bochum 113. 2 vols.

Stöllner, T. 2003. The economy of Dürrnberg-bei-Hallein: an Iron Age salt-mining centre in the Austrian Alps, *Antiquaries Journal* 83, 123-194.

Stopes, H. 1879. The salting mounds of Essex, *Archaeological Journal* 36, 369-372.

Szajnocha, W. 1891. *Źródła mineralne Galicji, pogląd na ich rozpołożenie, skład chemiczny i powstanie*. Kraków: Rozprawy Wydziału Matematyczno - Przyrodniczego Akademii Umiejętności.

Szajnocha, W. 1893. Kopalnie i warzelnie soli w Galicji, *Przewodnik Naukowy i Literacki* 21, Lwów.

Szentmiklosi, A., Heeb, B.S., Heeb, J., Harding, A., Krause, R. & Becker, H. 2011. Corneşti-Iarcuri - a Bronze Age town in the Romanian Banat?, *Antiquity* 85, 819-838.

Szombathy, J. 1900. Funde aus einem neu entdeckten vorgeschichtlichen Bergbau im Ender-Sinkwerk am Salzberg bei Hallstatt, *Mitteilungen der Anthropologischen Gesellschaft in Wien* 30, 203-5.

Tasić, N. 2000. Salt use in the Early and Middle Neolithic of the Balkan Peninsula. In: (ed) L. Nikolova, *Technology, Style and Society. Contributions to the innovations between the Alps and the Black Sea in prehistory*, 35-40. Oxford British Archaeological Reports, International Series 854.

Tasić, N. 2002. Salt trade in the Neolithic of south-east Europe. In: (ed) O. Weller, *Archéologie du sel: techniques et sociétés dans la pré- et protohistoire européenne / Salzarchäologie. Techniken und Gesellschaft in der Vor- und Frühgeschichte Europas*, 147-152. Rahden/Westf.: Marie Leidorf.

Terán Manrique, J. 2011. La producción de sal en la prehistoria de la Península Ibérica: estado de la cuestión, *@rqueología y Territorio* 8, 71-84.

Terán Manrique, J. & Morgado, A. 2011. El aprovechamiento prehistórico de sal en la Alta Andalucía. El caso de Fuente Camacho (Loja, Granada), *Cuadernos de Prehistoria y Arqueología de la Universidad de Granada* 21, 221-249.

Tessier, M. 1960. Découverte de gisements préhistoriques aux environs de la Pointe-Saint-Gildas, *Bulletin Société Préhistorique Française* 57, 428-34.

Thoen, H. 1975. Iron Age and Roman salt-making sites on the Belgian coast. In: (ed) K. W. De Brisay and K. A. Evans, *Salt. The study of an ancient industry, Report on the salt weekend*, 56-60. Colchester: Colchester Archaeological Group.

Thoen, H. 1990. La production du sel à l'époque celtique. In: (ed) G. Leman-Delerive, *Les Celtes en France du Nord et en Belgique, VIᵉ -Iᵉʳ siècle avant J.-C.: année de l'archéologie (Catalogue d'exposition, Musée des Beaux-Arts de Valenciennes)*, 282-290. Brussels: Crédit Communal.

Treml, M., Riepertinger, R. & Brockhoff, E. (ed) 1995. *Salz macht Geschichte. Aufsätze, Katalog*. Veröffentlichungen zu Bayerischen Geschichte und Kultur, 29/95 and 30/95. Augsburg: Haus der Bayerischen Geschichte.

Truong, M. 2003. *The Book of Salt*. Boston & New York: Mariner Books.

Ursulescu, N. 1977. Exploatarea sării din saramura în neoliticul timpuriu în lumina descoperirilor de la Solca (jud. Suceava), *Studii şi cercetări de istorie veche* 28/3, 307-317.

Valera, A.C., Tereso, J.P. & Rebuge, J. 2006. O Monte da Quinta 2 (Benevente) e a produçao de sal no Neolitico Final / Calcolitico do estuário do Tejo. In: (ed) N. Ferreira and H. Verissimo, *Actas do IV Congresso de Arqueologia Peninsular, Faro, setembro 2004*, 291-305. Faro: Universidade do Algarve.

Valiente Cánovas, S. & Ayanagüena Sanz, M. 2005. Cerámicas a mano utilizadas en la producción de la sal en las Salinas de Espartinas (Ciempozuelos, Madrid). In: (ed) O. Puche Riart and M. Ayarzagüena Sanz, *Minería y Metalurgia históricas en el Sudoeste Europeo*, 61-70. Madrid: SEDPGYM-SEHA.

Valiente Cánovas, S. & Ramos, P. 2009. Las salinas de Espartinas: un enclave prehistórico dedicado a la explotacíon de la sal. In: (ed) SEHA, *La explotacíon histórica de la sal: investigación y puesta en valor. Actas I Congreso Internacional Salinas de Espartinas, Ciempozuelos, 1 y 2 de diciembre de 2006*, 167-182. Madrid: Sociedad Española de Historia de la Arqueología. Memorias de la Sociedad Española de Historia de la Arqueología, II.

van den Broeke, P.W. 1995. Iron Age sea salt trade in the Lower Rhine area. In: (ed) J. D. Hill and C. G. Cumberpatch, *Different Iron Ages: Studies on the Iron Age in Temperate Europe*, 149-162. Oxford: British Archaeological Reports. BAR International Series 602.

van den Broeke, P.W. 1996. Southern sea salt in the Low Countries. A reconnaissance into the land of the Morini. In: (ed) M. Lodewijckx, *Archaeological and Historical Aspects of West-European Societies. Album amicorum André van Doorselaer*, 193-205. Leuven: Leuven University Press. Archaeologica Lovanensia, Monographiae 8.

van den Broeke, P.W. 2007. Zoutwinning langs de Noordzee: de pre-middeleeuwse sporen. In: (ed) A. M. J. de Kraker and G. J. Borger, *Veen-Vis-Zout. Landschappelijke dynamiek in de zuidwestelijke delta van de Lage Landen*, 65-80. Amsterdam: Vrije Universiteit. Geoarchaeological and Bioarchaeological Studies 8.

van der Leeuw, S. 1993. Giving the potter a choice: conceptual aspects of pottery techniques. In: (ed) P. Lemonnier, *Technological Choices. Transformation in material cultures since the Neolithic*, 238-288. London and New York: Routledge.

Vinski-Gasparini, K. 1973. *Kultura polja sa žarama u sjevernoj Hrvatskoj*. Zadar: Sveučilište u Zagrebu, Filozofski Fakultet - Zadar.

Vogt, U. 2003. Bemerkungen zur Technologie vorgeschichtlicher Salinen im Mittelgebirgsraum. In: (ed) T. Stöllner, G. Körlin, G. Steffens and J. Cierny, *Man and Mining. Mensch und Bergbau. Studies in Honour of Gerd Weisgerber on occasion of his 65th birthday*, 465-473. Bochum: Deutsches Bergbau-Museum. Der Anschnitt, Beiheft 16.

von Hochstetter, F. 1881. Ueber einen alten keltischen Bergbau im Salzberg von Hallstatt, *Mitteilungen der anthropologischen Gesellschaft in Wien* 11, 65-72.

von Rauchhaupt, R. & Schunke, T. 2010. Am Rande des Altsiedelgebietes. Archäologische Ausgrabungen an der Ortsumgehung Brehna, *Archäologie in Sachsen-Anhalt* Sonderband 12, 1-186.

Voss, A. 1901. Die Briquetage-Funde im Seillethal in Lothringen und ähnliche Funde in der Umgegend von Halle a.S. und im Saalethal, *Zeitschrift für Ethnologie, Verhandlungen* 33, 538-544.

Walter, H.-H. 1986. *3000 Jahre Salzgewinnung im Magdeburger Land*. Schönebeck (Elbe): Kreismuseum Schönebeck.

Weller, O. 2002a. Aux origines de la production du sel en Europe. Vestiges, fonctions et enjeux archéologiques. In: (ed) O. Weller, *Archéologie du sel: techniques et sociétés dans la pré- et protohistoire européenne / Salzarchäologie. Techniken und Gesellschaft in der Vor- und Frühgeschichte Europas*, 163-175. Rahden/Westf.: Verlag Marie Leidorf.

Weller, O. 2002b. The earliest rock salt exploitation in Europe: a salt mountain in the Spanish Neolithic, *Antiquity* 76, 317-318.

Weller, O. (ed) 2002c. Archéologie du sel: techniques et sociétés dans la pré- et protohistoire européenne / Salzarchäologie. Techniken und Gesellschaft in der Vor- und Frühgeschichte Europas. Internationale Archäologie: Arbeitsgemeinschaft, Symposium, Tagung, Kongress, Band 3. Rahden/Westf.: Verlag Marie Leidorf.

Weller, O. 2012. La production chalcolithique du sel à Provadia-Solnitsata: de la technologie céramique aux implications socio-économiques. In: (ed) V. Nikolov, *Salt and Gold: the role of salt in prehistoric Europe*, 67-87. Provadia / Veliko Tarnovo: Verlag Faber.

Weller, O., Dufraisse, A. & Pétrequin, P. (ed) 2008a. *Sel, eau et forêt. D'hier à aujourd'hui*. Collection "Les cahiers de la MSHE Ledoux", 12. Besançon: Presses universitaires de Franche-Comté.

Weller, O. & Dumitroaia, G. 2005. The earliest salt production in the world: an early Neolithic exploitation in *Poiana Slatinei*-Lunca, Romania, *Antiquity* 79, http://antiquity,ac.uk/ProjGall/weller/index.html, accessed 14/08/2007.

Weller, O., Dumitroaia, G., Sordoillet, D., Dufraisse, A., Gauthier, E. & Munteanu, R. 2008b. Première exploitation de sel en Europe. Techniques et gestion de l'exploitation de la source salée de Poiana Slatinei à Lunca (Neamţ, Roumanie). In: (ed) O. Weller, A. Dufraisse and P. Pétrequin, *Sel, eau et forêt. D'hier à aujourd'hui*, 205-230. Besançon: Presses universitaires de Franche-Comté. Collection "Les cahiers de la MSHE Ledoux", 12.

Weller, O., Dumitroaia, G., Sordoillet, D., Dufraisse, A., Gauthier, E. & Munteanu, R. 2009. Lunca-Poiana Slatinei (jud. Neamţ): cel mai vechi sit de exploatare a sării din preistoria europeană, *Arheologia Moldovei* 32, 21-39.

Weller, O. & Figuls, A. 2007. Première exploitation de sel gemme en Europe: organisation et enjeux socio-économiques au Néolithique moyen autour de *La Muntanya de Sal* de Cardona (Catalogne). In: (ed) A. Figuls and O. Weller, *1a Trobada internacional d'arqueologia envers l'explotació de la sal a la prehistòria i protohistòria, Cardona, 6-8 de desembre del 2003*, 219-239. Cardona: Institut de recerques envers la Cultura (IREC).

Wilkinson, T.J. & Murphy, P. 1986. Archaeological survey of an intertidal zone: the submerged landscape of the Essex coast, England, *Journal of Field Archaeology* 13, 177-94.

Wilkinson, T.J. & Murphy, P. 1995. *The Archaeology of the Essex Coast, I: The Hullbridge Survey*. Chelmsford: Archaeology Section, Essex County Council. East Anglian Archaeology 71.

Williams, E. 1999. The ethnoarchaeology of salt production at Lake Cuitzeo, Mexico, *Latin American Antiquity* 10, 400-414.

Williams, M. & Reid, M. 2008. *Salt: Life and Industry. Excavations at King Street, Middlewich, Cheshire, 2001-2002*. Oxford: Archaeopress. BAR British Series 456.

Willis, S. forthcoming. Chapter 12. The briquetage containers and salt networks in north-east England. In: (ed) C. C. Haselgrove, *Excavations and Fieldwork in the Tofts Field, Stanwick, North Yorkshire, 1984-2004*, York: Council for British Archaeology.

Windakiewicz, E. 1926. *Solnictwo, sole kamienne, potasowe i solanki, ich własności, fizjografia, górnictwo i warzelnictwo. vols I-IV*. Kraków: Skład Główny w Księgarni Jagiellońskiej.

Wollmann, V. 1996. *Mineritul metalifer, extragerea sării şi carierele de piatră în Dacia Romană / Der Erzbergbau, die Salzgewinnung und die Steinbrüche im Römischen Dakien*. Cluj-Napoca: Muzeul Naţional de Istorie a Transilvaniei. Bibliotheca Musei Napocensis 13 / Veröffentlichungen aus dem Deutschen Bergbau-Museum Bochum 63.

Woodiwiss, S. (ed) 1992. *Iron Age and Roman Salt Production and the Medieval Town of Droitwich*. CBA Research Report 81. London: Council for British Archaeology.

Żurowski, K. 1949 [1950]. Zabytki brązowe z młodszej epoki brązu i wczesnego okresu żelaza z dorzecza górnego Dniestru, *Przegląd Archeologiczny* 8, 155-247.